Mediterranean Meal Prep For Weight Loss

Rome .B Shannon

All rights reserved. Copyright © 2023 Rome .B Shannon

COPYRIGHT © 2023 Rome .B Shannon

All rights reserved.

No part of this book must be reproduced, stored in a retrieval system, or shared by any means, electronic, mechanical, photocopying, recording, or otherwise, without written permission from the publisher.

Every precaution has been taken in the preparation of this book; still the publisher and author assume no responsibility for errors or omissions. Nor do they assume any liability for damages resulting from the use of the information contained herein.

Legal Notice:

This book is copyright protected and is only meant for your individual use. You are not allowed to amend, distribute, sell, use, quote or paraphrase any of its part without the written consent of the author or publisher.

Introduction

This is a culinary guide that provides essential information about the Mediterranean diet and offers a variety of recipes to help readers get started on this healthy eating journey.

The cookbook begins by providing readers with an overview of what they should know about the Mediterranean diet, highlighting its benefits and principles. It emphasizes the use of fresh, whole ingredients, and explains how this dietary approach can promote overall well-being.

Following the introduction, the cookbook offers a selection of breakfast recipes, allowing readers to start their day with delicious and nutritious Mediterranean-inspired dishes. These breakfast recipes are designed to be both flavorful and healthy, incorporating ingredients like fruits, grains, and dairy products.

The cookbook then transitions to salad recipes, showcasing the versatility of Mediterranean cuisine when it comes to creating vibrant and satisfying salads. These recipes feature a variety of vegetables, grains, legumes, and dressings, catering to different tastes and preferences.

Next, the cookbook explores the world of soups and stews, providing recipes that are perfect for warming up on a cold day or enjoying as a hearty meal. These dishes often incorporate Mediterranean staples like tomatoes, beans, and aromatic herbs.

For those who enjoy poultry, seafood, and meat, the cookbook offers a range of recipes that celebrate these proteins while keeping in line with the Mediterranean diet's principles. These dishes feature lean cuts, flavorful marinades, and a focus on herbs and spices.

Vegetarians and appetizer enthusiasts will also find plenty to enjoy in this cookbook, as it includes a section dedicated to vegetarian recipes and appetizers. These dishes showcase the variety of flavors and textures that can be achieved with plant-based ingredients.

To help readers get started on their Mediterranean diet journey, the cookbook provides a 14-day meal plan. This plan offers a structured approach to incorporating Mediterranean-inspired meals into one's daily life, making it easier to adopt this healthy eating pattern.

Overall, this book is a comprehensive resource for those looking to embrace the Mediterranean diet. With a wide range of recipes, tips, and a 14-day meal plan, it offers a practical and flavorful introduction to this renowned and healthful way of eating.

Contents

Chapter One All You Should Know 1
Chapter Two Using the Mediterranean Diet 11
Chapter Three Recipes for Breakfast 16
Chapter Four Salad Recipes 41
Chapter Five Soup and Stews 54
Chapter Six Poultry, Seafood and Meat Recipes 85
Chapter Seven Vegetarian Recipes and Appetizers 138
14-Day Meal Plan 156

Chapter One All You Should Know

The Mediterranean diet is undoubtedly something you've heard of unless you've been hiding out. In recent years, this diet has attracted a lot of attention—and for good reason. The most nutrient-dense and useful diet now accessible is the Mediterranean diet, sometimes referred to as the heart-healthy diet.

When we look more carefully at the Mediterranean diet, we see that it is less of a traditional diet and more of a way of life and culinary history for the people who live there. The staples include whole grains, fresh fruits and vegetables, fish, nuts, olive oil, and the sporadic glass of wine.

The Mediterranean diet is founded on a culture that values using the freshest ingredients, preparing food simply yet delightfully, and enjoying it in a casual atmosphere with friends and family.

Though most of us understand its importance for better health and a higher quality of life, few of us really follow it. Since we spend the most of our days at work, we like to go for quick and straightforward options when it comes to meals. We often reach for fast food, prepared meals from the grocery store, and processed foods first.

Since all varieties of food are now available year-round, people all around the globe have stopped consuming seasonal cuisine. Furthermore, creating meals from scratch seems like an unnecessary hassle considering our jam-packed schedules and the time it takes to prepare a great dinner.

Therefore, rather than eating foods that develop as plants, we eat meals that are generated by plants. Our diets are defined by overly processed foods, unhealthy fats, copious amounts of sugar, and a slew of man-made ingredients with names most of us can't even pronounce.

One of the best things about the Mediterranean diet is how easy and basic it is. As our recipes section will show, you don't need to be a master chef to make delectable food. Eat more fish, particularly oily fish rich in omega-3 fatty acids, cook with extra virgin olive oil, and consume a variety of fresh produce, whole grains, nuts, and cereals throughout the day.

The Mediterranean diet places a strong emphasis on the consumption of healthy fats such olive oil, fish, avocado, nuts, and seeds, in contrast to many other popular diets. A few glasses of red wine a year may also help lower your risk of cardiovascular disease.

Consider the following for a brief summary of the Mediterranean diet:

Eat only plant-based foods.

Your meals should be built around fresh and organic fruits, vegetables, legumes, nuts, and beans. Your body will get high-quality nutrition from these whole foods in the form of fiber-rich complex carbs that digest slowly, antioxidants, vitamins, and phytochemicals.

Furthermore, these meals will keep you satisfied for longer due to their high fiber content, stopping you from snacking on unhealthy foods and providing you with disease-fighting nutrition.

Consume just whole grains.

Avoid refined grain items that have lost most of their healthful components, such as white rice and bleached white flour. Choose whole grain alternatives instead, such as oats, brown rice, whole wheat, bulgur, farro, barley, quinoa, millet, and corn. Compared to processed grains, whole grains are higher in fiber, minerals, and vitamins.

Eat fish or shellfish at least two times every week.

Fish and shellfish are low in saturated fat and provide your body the essential omega-3 fatty acids. Popular fish and shellfish in the Mediterranean cuisine include clams, anchovies, salmon, mussels, bream, octopus, sardines, shrimp, herring, crab, squid, tuna, and sea bass.

Make sure you only purchase wild-caught fish to avoid the mercury contamination common in farmed fish.

sometimes consume very little quantities of red meat.

Red meat has a lot of saturated fat. Despite being a component of the Mediterranean diet due to its health benefits, it should only be consumed seldom.

As little as feasible, limit your dairy consumption to cheese and yogurt.

Cheese and natural yogurt are very nutrient-dense components of the Mediterranean diet when consumed in moderation. These ensure that you get enough calcium to maintain healthy bones. Probiotics are another ingredient in yogurt that aid in digestion by supplying your stomach with healthy bacteria.

Healthy fats may be found in foods like olives, avocados, fatty seafood, nuts, seeds, and extra virgin olive oil.

Monounsaturated fats and antioxidants, which are excellent for your heart, are abundant in olives and olive oil. Olives are great as a snack or in pasta dishes, stews, and salads. Unsaturated fats are abundant in avocado as well. It tastes great on its own, in a smoothie, or in a salad.

Almonds, walnuts, hazelnuts, cashews, pine nuts, sesame seeds, and pumpkin seeds are just a few examples of the nuts and seeds that contain healthy fats.

Avoid trans fats like those in margarine or hydrogenated oils as well as saturated fats like those in cream, butter, lard, and red meat.

every so often, have a glass of red wine.

Red wine may benefit your heart by raising the levels of healthy cholesterol when drank in moderation (HDL). This is because red wine contains antioxidants.

Balance is the key.

Although theoretically there are no restricted foods, it's important to monitor your intake, especially when eating foods high in calories and saturated fat. Consume as much natural and nutritious food as you can to improve your health.

Spend some time having fun and being active.

The Mediterranean lifestyle is more laid-back than the typical western way of living. Meals with friends and family are quite popular in the Mediterranean region. Most people walk or ride their bikes to work instead of driving, and they take more vacations, which lowers stress.

The Mediterranean culture is characterized by a cuisine that is abundant in scents, hues, and wonderful recollections, supporting the spirit—and palate—of people who are in touch with nature.

The Mediterranean diet has long been a topic of conversation, but few people really adhere to it. While some people link the Mediterranean diet to pasta and meat sauce, others link it to pizza. In this book, we'll examine the history of the Mediterranean diet to get a deeper grasp of its components.

The Mediterranean region, dubbed "The Cradle of Society" since it was the setting for the whole of ancient history, is where this heart-healthy diet originated.

The origins of the Mediterranean diet, however, have been lost to the passage of time. We may go back to the eating customs and patterns of the Middle Ages or even farther to Roman civilisation (which was a copy of Greek civilization) and their identification of red wine, bread, and oil as indicators of their rural way of life.

Many people in the Mediterranean region fished, farmed fruits and vegetables, and farmed the soil. Because of the unfavorable grazing conditions, beef and dairy products were not very common in this region. Fish, goats, and lamb were the most often used protein sources.

The scientific foundation of the Mediterranean diet.

There is a reason why the Mediterranean diet is sometimes called the "heart-healthy diet" With modest quantities of fatty fish and dairy products, minimal meat, saturated fat, and sugar, this diet has traditionally been high in fresh fruits and vegetables, grains, and legumes.

The vast bulk of the fat in this diet is provided by olive oil, avocado, salmon, nuts, and seeds. Alcohol is used in moderation, usually in the form of red wine.

According to a 1960s scientific research that gave origin to the "heart-healthy" diet, men who consumed a traditional Mediterranean diet had fewer heart attacks.

Additional studies have linked the Mediterranean diet to a lower risk of heart attack, stroke, type 2 diabetes, and early death from illness. It has also been shown that adhering to the principles of the Mediterranean diet improves cognitive function.

The results of a thorough analysis done to see how the Mediterranean diet affected dementia were positive. Significant amounts of antioxidants are provided by fresh fruits and vegetables, as well as the occasional glass of red wine, in the Mediterranean diet. These antioxidants may increase the amounts of proteins in the brain that protect brain cells from injury and may also help protect brain cells from damage brought on by Alzheimer's disease.

Inflammation is the root cause of Alzheimer's disease, and the Mediterranean diet is a powerful anti-inflammatory diet. For many of us, adopting a Mediterranean diet is the finest kind of health insurance we can get.

The Mediterranean diet may lengthen your life.

A Mediterranean diet is undoubtedly one of the keys to enduring vitality because of its fresh, healthy, natural, nourishing, and healthful dietary composition. You'll see a change in your appearance and level of energy as soon as you begin this diet. To enhance your future health, begin a Mediterranean diet now.

What advantages does a Mediterranean diet have?

Low in sugar alternatives and processed foods.

In the Mediterranean diet, foods like olive oil, peas, legumes, fruits, nuts, seeds, vegetables, and unprocessed whole grain products are examples of foods that are very close to their natural state. Wild-caught seafood is another well-liked option to plant-based diets, with sardines, salmon, and anchovies being the most popular. As a source of calcium, good fats, and cholesterol, it is advised to consume goat, cow, or sheep cheeses and yogurt in moderation.

Despite the fact that the majority of people in the Mediterranean region are not vegetarians, this cuisine promotes a minimal consumption of meat. Make better decisions that will help you lose weight and enhance your health.

Long-lasting, healthy weight reduction.

If you want to lose weight without feeling deprived and keep the weight off for the rest of your life, this is the plan for you. This diet has helped a lot of people lose weight and improve their overall health since it naturally eliminates processed foods and unhealthy fats by placing a greater emphasis on plant-based foods.

The Mediterranean diet also allows for interpretation, whether you choose a low-protein, low-carb, or somewhere in between diet. The Mediterranean diet places a strong emphasis on consuming fruits, vegetables, healthy fats, and lean protein.

Enhances the condition of your heart.

Olive oil is important in the Mediterranean diet. Olive oil contains the molecule alpha-linoleic acid, which has been shown to reduce the frequency of fatal cardiac events by up to 45%.

By reducing high blood pressure and levels of bad cholesterol, the Mediterranean diet, which includes omega-3 and monounsaturated fats, has been demonstrated to reduce heart disease-related mortality.

This prevents cancer.

The olive oil, fruit, vegetables, and wine that make up the Mediterranean diet provide a balanced amount of omega-3 and omega-6 essential fats, as well as fiber, vitamins, antioxidants, minerals, and polyphenols.

This antioxidant-rich diet assists in the fight against cancer by protecting your DNA, reducing inflammation, stopping cell mutation, and delaying the growth of tumors. The prevalence of bowel and colon cancer has also been related to olive oil use.

Diabetes is avoided and its symptoms are lessened.

The Mediterranean diet is the ideal anti-inflammatory diet due to its focus on organic and natural foods. Chronic diseases like type 2 diabetes, which are associated with chronic inflammation, may be treated with the use of this anti-inflammatory property.

By regulating insulin levels, the Mediterranean diet assists in the prevention of diabetes. The hormone insulin, which controls blood sugar levels, makes people gain weight and stores sugar and other carbohydrates as fat.

When you regulate your blood sugar levels with a healthy diet, your body becomes more efficient at burning fat. This lowers your blood sugar levels while also assisting in weight loss.

Enhances mental clarity and mood.

If strictly followed, this heart-healthy diet may help prevent and reduce the symptoms of Parkinson's disease, dementia, and Alzheimer's disease. Problems emerge when your brain receives insufficient nutrition to support the generation of dopamine, a hormone essential for mood regulation, proper movement, and thought processing.

The superior nutrition of the Mediterranean diet guards against the damaging effects of pollutants and helps to stave against age-related cognitive decline.

Longevity.

If you consume a fresh, nourishing, natural, organic, and healthful meal, every function in your body will be operating at full efficiency, providing you increased energy to carry out your daily chores. Both your skin and hair will become better. You will be in flawless condition throughout!

Calming and an excellent way to reduce stress.

The Mediterranean way of life encourages you to spend quality time with nature and the people you care about, such as family and friends, in addition to focusing on your diet. There is no better way to spend quality time with your family than while enjoying a delicious and healthy home-cooked meal served outdoors while telling jokes and doing what you all like. even a dance, maybe! There is nothing better than a bottle of red wine after a family supper.

A lifestyle that will improve your overall health, promote weight reduction, and help you find balance in your life is the Mediterranean diet. You will learn to appreciate nature and all that it has to offer.

Take advantage of the ample food this season has to offer and start enjoying this heart-healthy supper rich in antioxidants, unsaturated fats, vitamins, and minerals. You may even light up your grill while following this Mediterranean-style weight-loss plan, enjoying the tastiest cuisine and a slimmer you!

Fruits and vegetables provide you the energy you need to refrain from consuming junk food.

If you are lacking in antioxidants, phytochemicals, and micronutrients like vitamins and minerals, you won't be able to lose weight. When we are weary, we are more tempted to eat junk food, but studies show that the micronutrients in fruits and vegetables boost metabolism and provide your body with high-quality, clean energy.

Dehydration and hunger are often confused. You can find yourself chewing on the adjacent meal when all you needed was a lovely glass of water. Over 90% of the water in most vegetables helps prevent even slight dehydration, which might decrease your body's ability to burn fat.

Extra virgin olive oil contains the highest content of monounsaturated fat when compared to other meals and oils. Your energy levels will improve if you consume more olive oil and less saturated fat, which is the first thing you'll notice. Additionally, in order to maintain your energy levels, you will burn more fat.

Furthermore, smelling olive oil before meals may aid in reducing appetite. Use olive oil in place of butter on toast, in salad dressings, and in cooking to lose weight more quickly and sustainably.

The ideal bacteria for fat burning are present in natural Greek yogurt.

The amount of protein per ounce in this yogurt is greater than that of other ready-to-eat meals. As a result, it prevents overeating, curbs cravings, keeps blood sugar levels stable, and keeps you satisfied for a longer period of time.

Additionally, protein metabolism uses more energy than carbohydrate metabolism. Probiotics, which assist to fill your stomach with good bacteria that fight bacteria, germs, viruses, and sickness, are another healthy component of Greek yogurt.

Legumes are a necessary source of both types of fiber for weight reduction.

Soluble and insoluble fiber are essential for weight loss. Of all the foods on earth, legumes offer the finest combination of the two.

When soluble fiber dissolves in the liquids of your stomach, it turns into a gel-like substance. This increases your feeling of fullness while keeping food in your stomach for a longer period of time, which slows down digestion.

Contrarily, insoluble fiber absorbs water and increases the volume of your digestive tract. You won't feel the want to snack on junk food as much since digestion is delayed.

Seafood speeds up the process of burning fat.

Omega-3 fatty acids are crucial for blood sugar sensitivity, metabolism, and any other system involved in fat burning, yet many Americans are not receiving enough of them.

Cold-water fatty fish like salmon, herring, and sardines have greater levels of omega-3 fatty acids than leaner fish. The most potent omega-3 fatty acids, EPA/DHA omega-3 lipids, are found in seafood.

Following the Mediterranean diet's advice to eat fish and shellfish will increase your metabolism by up to 400 calories per day and stop fat cells from forming, especially around your stomach.

Chapter Two Using the Mediterranean Diet

We've shown so far that the Mediterranean diet is not a trendy eating plan with a catchy name that guarantees rapid weight reduction. It's a sensible way to eat and live that will improve your health, lifestyle, and general well-being.

This diet is very doable and easy to follow since it doesn't restrict any significant food groups. It is also a reasonably priced diet to follow. Let's look at a straightforward approach to beginning this heart-healthy diet.

Failure to plan is planning failure.

There are little changes you can do to improve your life, and they start with developing a clear plan that involves goal-setting. On the other side, establishing goals is typically the easiest part; achieving them may be challenging.

Do things gradually at start.

Focus on reaching one goal at a time while taking little, deliberate actions. Start with a target you know you can hit every day for the next week, such as eating fresh vegetables at every meal or getting up when your alarm goes off without hitting the snooze button.

Being successful includes creating a new, healthy habit in addition to accomplishing a goal. Once you've established one healthy habit, what's to stop you from creating more?

You should be motivated by deadlines, and you should record them often.

Your "I want" will become a "I did it!" with deadlines!

Writing down each deadline strengthens your self-commitment and provides your goals a feeling of urgency.

The principles of the Mediterranean diet are now clear to you. You'll be well on your way to excellent health if you pair them with a regular exercise schedule.

The Mediterranean diet will quickly become second nature to you if you keep things in perspective and take each day as it comes.

Success techniques.

The USDA and Mediterranean food pyramids should be compared and contrasted.

The Mediterranean diet places a high priority on fruits, vegetables, legumes, whole grains, olive oil, natural herbs, and spices. It also recommends eating fish and shellfish once or twice a week, as well as eggs, poultry, cheese, yogurt, red meat, and wine in moderation.

The Mediterranean diet pyramid allows for less red meat, sweet fruits, and dairy as compared to the USDA's food pyramid. It also permits a larger intake of healthy fats and oils.

No matter how busy your day is, make time for breakfast every morning.

As you well know, breakfast is the most important meal of the day. The word "breakfast," which derives from the phrase "break the fast." refers to the breaking of the all-night fast. Your day will start out with a boost of energy from a nutrient-dense breakfast made up of fruits, vegetables, whole grains, and other fiber-rich foods. This breakfast will also keep you full until your next meal.

Recognize the difference between healthy and unhealthy fats. Monounsaturated fats, which are healthy fats, may be found in foods like almonds, sunflower seeds, avocados, extra virgin olive oil, and olives.

The polyunsaturated oils found in soybean, sunflower, maize, and safflower oils are also healthy fats. These improve heart health and lower harmful cholesterol.

Contrarily, unhealthy fats like trans and saturated fats may boost your bad cholesterol levels and increase your chance of developing heart disease if you eat too much of them.

Vegetables should be a major component of every meal.

Vegetables high in fiber help you feel fuller for longer and have better digestion. Add fresh vegetables, herbs, and spices to your omelets, pizza, soups, stews, sandwiches, and other meals.

Cut down on your meat intake.

Did you know that Americans are the world's biggest meat consumers? This may help to explain why we are one of the world's fattest countries, if not the fattest.

Reduce your diet of red meat to minimize your intake of saturated and trans fats found in animal products.

You can sometimes eat red meat, but only in moderation and only from lean cuts.

Eat fish and seafood at least twice every week.

Fish including salmon, tuna, sardines, and herring are rich sources of omega-3 fatty acids. Oysters, mussels, and clams are shellfish that have heart- and brain-healthy qualities. To make meals interesting, try experimenting with new recipes, such as those we'll present in our recipes area.

Set a regular time aside for family meals.

The Mediterranean diet is founded on cultures that value quality time with loved ones above scrumptious and nutritious meals and drinks.

Most of us are unable to partake in a family meal where we can all eat and laugh together due to our hectic schedules. This is important for the wellbeing of your family as well as for yourself. Eating meals as a family makes your relationships stronger as you enjoy good food.

Stay active.

No matter how busy you are, find time to play with your kids, take a walk around the block, work out, or take dancing lessons. whatsoever kind of exercise you like. DON'T WAIT! You should make a commitment to working out for at least 30 minutes each day.

For a fit body, get up from your desk or couch and walk about.

Consuming a Mediterranean-style diet

The Mediterranean diet is not a one-size-fits-all system. This diet is not a "one size fits all" strategy, as shown by the fact that people in various Mediterranean countries consume a variety of foods.

What precisely are the tasks on your list?

The aim is to consistently pile plant-based foods on your plate, with fruits and vegetables taking up the majority of the area. Eat red meat sometimes and fish two to three times every week. You should also include high-nutrient whole grains and legumes in your diet.

A great snack is nuts and seeds, which you should always cook with extra virgin olive oil.

The most crucial beverage for a Mediterranean diet is water, which you should have eight glasses of each day. Additionally good for your heart is a glass of red wine with dinner!

A list of foods to buy for a Mediterranean diet.

Always choose meals that are as little processed as possible, giving preference to fresh, organic veggies. You'll often locate whole foods near the supermarket's perimeter, so it's best to explore there.

As a general rule, get rid of everything unhealthy from your kitchen that isn't a part of the Mediterranean diet, such crackers, refined grain products, sodas, and other artificially sweetened beverages.

You will consume nutritious meals if it is the only option you have at home. Consuming something that isn't there is impossible!

Here are some recommendations for meals that fit the Mediterranean diet.

- It's easy to follow the Mediterranean diet while eating out.
- Pick fish or seafood for your main dish.
- Make sure that extra virgin olive oil is used to fry all of your vegetables and food.
- Use whole-grain bread brushed with extra virgin olive oil in place of butter. Pour a glass of red wine and some berries or grapes for dessert.
- After going through every essential component of the Mediterranean diet, it's time to move on to the exciting part: the food.

Chapter Three
Recipes for Breakfast

Paninis with cream.

Time to cook: 5 minutes

Approximately 4 servings

Ingredients:

- 1/4 cup chopped fresh basil leaves 2 tablespoons coarsely chopped black olives, oil-cured
- split half cup mayonnaise dressing with olive oil 8 whole-wheat bread slices
- four bacon slices
- 1 finely sliced small zucchini 4 provolone cheese slices
- 7 oz. sliced roasted red peppers

Directions:

- Combine the olives, basil, and 1/4 cup mayonnaise in a small dish; spread the mayonnaise mixture equally on the bread slices and stack 4 pieces with bacon, zucchini, provolone, and peppers.
- Spread the remaining quarter cup of mayonnaise over the exterior of the sandwiches and cook for approximately 4 minutes, flipping once, until the cheese is melted and the sandwiches are golden brown.

Couscous for breakfast.

Time to cook: 5 minutes

Approximately 4 servings

Ingredients:

- 1 cinnamon stick (2 inches) 3 cups 1 percent fat-free milk
- 1 cup couscous (whole wheat) (uncooked) split 6 teaspoons dark brown sugar
- dried currants, quarter cup
- half a cup apricots, chopped (dried)
- a quarter teaspoon of salt
- 4 tablespoons melted butter

Directions:

- Combine cinnamon stick and milk in a saucepan over medium high heat; cook for 3 minutes (do not boil).
- Take the pan off the heat and add the couscous, 4 tablespoons sugar, currants, apricots, and sea salt. Allow the mixture to sit for at least 15 minutes, covered.
- Remove the cinnamon stick and divide the couscous among four dishes; sprinkle half a teaspoon of sugar and 1 teaspoon melted butter over each meal.
- Serve right away.

Hash with potatoes and chickpeas.

Time to cook: 5 minutes

Approximately 4 servings

Ingredients:

- 4 cups frozen hash brown potatoes, shredded 1 tablespoon ginger, freshly minced
- 1/2 cup onion, chopped
- 2 cups baby spinach, chopped a tablespoon of curry powder
- a half teaspoon of salt
- extra virgin olive oil, quarter cup 15-ounce can chickpeas, washed 1 cup sliced zucchini a dozen big eggs

Directions:

- Combine the potatoes, ginger, onion, spinach, curry powder, and sea salt in a large mixing basin.
- Heat extra virgin olive oil in a nonstick pan over medium high heat before adding the potato mixture.
- Cook for approximately 5 minutes, stirring occasionally, or until golden brown and crispy.
- Reduce the heat to low and stir in the zucchini and chickpeas, breaking up the mixture as needed.
- Make four wells by stirring slightly and pressing the mixture back into a layer. In each indentation, crack one egg.
- Cook for 5 minutes, covered, or until eggs are set.

Toast with avocado.

Time to cook: 0 minutes

Approximately 4 servings

Ingredients:

- peeled ripe avocados
- fresh lemon juice squeezed to taste
- 2 tbsp mint, freshly cut, with additional to garnish to taste with sea salt and black pepper
- 4 big rye bread slices
- 80 grams crumbled soft feta

Directions:

- Mash the avocado with a fork in a medium bowl; add the lemon juice and mint and mash until just incorporated.
- To taste, season with black pepper and sea salt. Toast or grill the bread till golden.
- Top each piece of toasted bread with a quarter of the avocado mixture and feta cheese.
- Serve immediately with additional mint as a garnish.

Pancakes with a Mediterranean flair.

Time to prepare: 20 minutes

Ingredients:

- 1 cup oats, old-fashioned
- 1/2 cup flour (all-purpose) 2 tablespoons flaxseed
- 1 teaspoon baking soda
- a quarter teaspoon of salt
- extra virgin olive oil, 1 tablespoon 2 big eggs 1 cup plain nonfat Greek yogurt 2 tablespoons raw honey

- Fruit, syrup, or other garnishes

Directions:

- Blend oats, flour, flax seeds, baking soda, and sea salt for roughly 30 seconds in a blender.
- Pulse in the extra virgin olive oil, eggs, yogurt, and honey until completely smooth.
- Allow at least 20 minutes for the mixture to thicken.
- Brush a large nonstick skillet with extra virgin olive oil and place it over medium heat.
- Ladle the batter into the pan in quarter-cupfuls in batches.
- Cook for approximately 2 minutes, or until bubbles appear and the pancakes are golden brown.
- Cook for a further 2 minutes or until golden brown on the opposite side.
- Place the cooked pancakes on a baking sheet in the oven to keep warm.
- Serve with your preferred toppings.

Frittata Mediterranean.

15 minutes to prepare.

Approximately 4 servings

Ingredients:

- 1 tablespoon extra virgin olive oil 1 cup onion, chopped

- 2 garlic cloves, minced ¼ cup half-and-half, milk or light cream 8 eggs, beaten
- half a cup Kalamata olives, sliced
- half cup chopped roasted red sweet peppers half cup feta cheese crumbles
- 1/4 cup fresh basil 1/8 teaspoon black pepper
- ½ cup coarsely smashed onion-and-garlic croutons 2 tbsp. Parmesan cheese, finely grated To garnish, fresh basil leaves

Directions:

- Preheat the oven's broiler.
- In a broiler-proof pan placed over medium heat, heat 2 tablespoons extra virgin olive oil; sauté onion and garlic for a few minutes or until soft.
- Meanwhile, whisk together the eggs and half-and-half in a mixing dish.
- Combine the olives, roasted sweet pepper, feta cheese, black pepper, and basil in a mixing bowl.
- Cook until the egg mixture is nearly set over the sautéed onion mixture.
- Lift the egg mixture with a spatula to let the uncooked portion to run below.
- Cook for another 2 minutes or until the set is achieved.
- In a small dish, combine the remaining extra virgin olive oil, Parmesan cheese, and smashed croutons; sprinkle over the frittata and broil for 5 minutes, or until the crumbs are brown and the top has set.

- Cut the frittata into wedges and serve with fresh basil on top.

Oatmeal with Nutty Bananas.

Time to cook: 5 minutes

Approximately 4 servings

Ingredients:

- quarter cup oats (quick cooking) 3 tablespoons raw honey
- a half gallon of skim milk
- 2 tablespoons walnuts, chopped 1 teaspoon flaxseed
- 1 peeled banana

Directions:

- Combine oats, honey, milk, walnuts, and flaxseeds in a microwave-safe bowl; microwave on high for 2 minutes.
- Mash the banana with a fork to a fine consistency in a small dish; add into the oats and serve hot.

Omelet with Mediterranean Veggies

Time to prepare: 25 minutes.

Approximately 4 servings

Ingredients:

- cup thinly sliced fresh fennel bulb quarter cup chopped artichoke hearts, soaked in water, drained quarter cup pitted green olives, brine-cured, chopped 1 Roma tomato, diced
- 6 eggs
- half teaspoon freshly ground black pepper quarter teaspoon sea salt
- ½ cup crumbled goat cheese
- 2 tbsp. fresh parsley, dill, or basil, chopped

Directions:

- Preheat the oven to 325 degrees Fahrenheit.
- In an ovenproof skillet, heat extra virgin olive oil over medium heat. Fennel should be cooked for 5 minutes or until soft.
- Cook for 3 minutes or until artichoke hearts, olives, and tomatoes are softened.
- In a mixing dish, whisk together the eggs and season with salt and pepper.
- Stir for approximately 2 minutes after pouring the egg mixture over the veggies. Sprinkle cheese on top of the omelet and bake for 5 minutes, or until it is set and cooked through.
- Sprinkle with parsley, dill, or basil before serving.
- Place the omelet on a cutting board and cut it into four wedges. Serve right away.

Scones with lemon.

15 minutes to prepare.

Approximately 12 servings

Ingredients:

- 2 cups flour plus a quarter cup
- a half teaspoon of baking soda 2 tablespoons sugar
- a half teaspoon of salt
- 34 cup low-fat buttermilk 1 lemon's zest to 2 teaspoons freshly squeezed lemon juice 1 cup sugar powder

Directions:

- Preheat the oven to 400 degrees Fahrenheit.
- Combine 2 cups flour, baking soda, sugar, and salt in a food processor and mix until smooth.
- Mix in the buttermilk and lemon zest until everything is properly combined. Turn out the dough onto a clean surface and gently knead it at least six times before shaping it into a ball.
- Flatten the dough with a rolling pin into a half-inch thick circle.
- Cut the dough into four equal wedges, then three smaller wedges from each.
- Place the scones on a baking sheet and bake for 15 minutes or until golden brown in a preheated oven.
- In a separate bowl, combine the lemon juice and powdered sugar to form a thin frosting.
- While still hot, remove the scones from the oven and pour with lemon icing.

- Serve immediately.

Wrapped Breakfast

Time to cook: 5 minutes

Approximately 2 servings

Ingredients:

- half cup spinach, freshly harvested 4 beaten egg whites
- Sun-dried tomatoes Bella 2 flax wraps with mixed grains
- feta cheese crumbles (half cup)

Directions:

- In a frying pan, cook spinach, egg whites, and tomatoes for approximately 4 minutes, or until gently browned.
- Cook for another 4 minutes or until nearly done on the other side. Remove the wraps from the microwave and fill each with the egg mixture, feta cheese crumbles, and roll them up.
- Serve by dividing each wrap into two halves.

Scrambled Eggs with Garlic.

15 minutes of cooking time

Approximately 2 servings

Ingredients:

- extra virgin olive oil, half a teaspoon

- half a pound of ground beef
- a half teaspoon of garlic powder 3 eggs
- seasonings

Directions:

- Preheat a medium-sized skillet over medium-high heat.
- Heat the extra virgin olive oil until it is warm but not smoking.
- Cook for approximately 10 minutes, or until the ground beef is nearly done.
- Sauté for approximately 2 minutes after adding the garlic.
- Beat the eggs in a large mixing bowl until nearly foamy; season with salt and pepper.
- Scramble the egg mixture in the pan with the cooked meat until it is done.
- For a nutritious and filling breakfast, serve with toasted bread and olives.

Breakfast Casserole with Fruit.

Time to cook: 50 minutes

Approximately 6 servings

- Ingredients:
- 2 tablespoons extra virgin olive oil, halved medium onion, chopped medium yellow potatoes diced 1

pound zucchini, chopped portabella mushroom caps, 1 pound zucchini 150g fresh spinach, torn

- Ricotta cheese (200g)
- 200g ricotta cheese (light) egg whites, 2 cups
- 12 grape tomatoes, cut into thirteen pieces 3 fresh peppers, peeled and roasted, sliced 2 rolls (sourdough)
- 100g skim-milk mozzarella cheese, shredded 4 tablespoons Pecorino Romano

Directions:

- Preheat the oven to 400 degrees Fahrenheit.
- Roast for at least 15 minutes with olive oil, onion, and potato; remove from oven and keep on baking pan.
- Combine half tablespoon olive oil and zucchini in a mixing bowl; toss to coat thoroughly and transfer to a baking pan.
- Return all of the veggies to the oven and roast for 40 minutes, or until golden.
- Meanwhile, heat half a tablespoon of olive oil in a skillet and cook mushrooms for 4 minutes.
- Set aside the cooked mushrooms from the pan.
- Sauté the chopped spinach in the remaining olive oil until soft.
- Combine both kinds of ricotta and egg whites in a mixing basin; leave aside.
- In a 9 x 13 baking dish, combine all of the veggies, including grape tomatoes and peppers, with the

sourdough rolls; top with the ricotta mixture and pecorino and mozzarella cheese.

- Bake until done, at least 40 minutes. Remove from the oven and set aside to cool.
- Enjoy your breakfast by cutting it into six pieces.

Breakfast Casserole with Eggs and Sausage

1 hour and 5 minutes to cook

Approximately 12 servings

Ingredients:

The topping:

- 2 pound peeled and shredded russet potatoes 3 tablespoons olive oil
- 34 teaspoon powdered pepper 34 teaspoon salt

The chowder:

- 12 oz. turkey sausage, chopped ¼ cup diced bell pepper 4 finely sliced green onions
- 13 gallon skim milk 6 eggs, big
- 4 beaten egg whites
- 34 cup cheddar cheese, shredded Cottage cheese, low-fat, 16 ounces

Directions:

The topping:

- Preheat the oven to 425 degrees Fahrenheit. Set aside a 913-inch baking dish lightly greased with 1 tablespoon olive oil.

- Using a kitchen towel or paper towel, wring off any extra liquid from the potato.
- In a medium bowl, toss the potatoes with the remaining olive oil, salt, and pepper until evenly covered.
- Bake for approximately 20 minutes, or until golden brown around the edges, in a greased baking dish.

The chowder:

- Preheat the oven to 375°F.
- Cook turkey sausage in a big pan over medium-high heat for approximately 2 minutes, or until it's nearly done.
- Add the green onions and red bell pepper and sauté for another 2 minutes, or until the bell pepper is soft.
- Skim milk, eggs, egg whites, and cheeses are whisked together.
- Pour over the potato crust and bake for approximately 50 minutes, stirring in the turkey sausage mixture. Allow it cool slightly before cutting into 12 pieces. Enjoy!

Pancakes with Yogurt.

Time to cook: 5 minutes

Approximately 5 servings

Ingredients:

- pancake mix made with whole wheat 1 quart of yogurt

- 1 tablespoon of baking powder 1 teaspoon of baking soda
- 1 quart skim milk 3 eggs (whole)
- extra virgin olive oil, half a teaspoon

Directions:

- In a large mixing bowl, combine whole-wheat pancake mix, yogurt, baking powder, baking soda, skimmed milk, and eggs.
- Stir until everything is completely combined.
- Warm a pan lightly greased with olive oil.
- Pour a quarter cup of batter into the hot pan and cook for 2 minutes, or until bubbles appear on the top of the pancake.
- Cook until the underside is browned before flipping.
- With a cup of fat-free milk or two teaspoons light maple syrup, serve the pancakes warm.

Stir-fried breakfast.

Time to cook: 20 minutes

Approximately 4 servings

Ingredients:

- extra virgin olive oil, 1 tablespoon
- 2 green peppers, diced
- 4 tomatoes, chopped
- 1/2 teaspoon sea salt

- 1 egg

Directions:

- In a medium-sized pan, heat the olive oil over medium-high heat. Add the green pepper and cook for 2 minutes.
- Reduce the heat to medium and cook for another 3 minutes, covered.
- Cook for approximately 2 minutes, or until the onion is golden.
- Stir in the tomatoes and salt, then cover and cook until the mixture is soft and moist.
- Beat the egg in a bowl; sprinkle over the tomato mixture and simmer for 1 minute. (Do not mix.)
- For a delicious breakfast, top with diced cucumbers, feta cheese, and black olives.

Pitas for Greek Breakfast

Time to prepare: 10 minutes

Approximately 4 servings

Ingredients:

- 1/4 cup onion, chopped
- ¼ cup chopped sweet red/black pepper 1 big egg, 1 cup
- 18 teaspoon salt
- 1/8 teaspoon black pepper

- half cup baby spinach, freshly torn half teaspoon fresh basil, crushed 2 tbsp. feta cheese, crumbled 1 red tomato, sliced pita bread

Directions:

- Cook over medium heat in a large nonstick skillet coated with cooking spray.
- Sauté for at least 3 minutes with the onions and red peppers.
- Combine the egg, pepper, and salt in a small dish and pour into the skillet.
- Cook until done, stirring constantly.
- Top the pitas with basil, spinach, and tomatoes before adding the egg mixture.
- Serve with feta cheese on top.

Scrambled Eggs for Breakfast

15 minutes to prepare.

Approximately 2 servings

Ingredients:

- 1 tablespoon extra virgin olive oil
- 4 chopped medium green onions
- 1 teaspoon dried basil leaves or 1 tablespoon minced fresh basil leaves 4 eggs 1 medium tomato, diced
- pepper, freshly ground

Directions:

- Heat olive oil in a medium nonstick pan over medium heat; cook green onions for approximately 2 minutes, turning periodically.
- Stir in the basil and tomato and heat for approximately 1 minute, or until the tomato is cooked through, stirring periodically.
- With a wire whisk or a fork, thoroughly beat the eggs in a small basin and pour over the tomato mixture; simmer for approximately 2 minutes.
- To enable the uncooked pieces to flow to the bottom, gently lift the cooked parts with a spatula.
- Cook for another 3 minutes, or until the eggs are fully cooked.
- Serve with a pinch of black pepper.

Greek Salad.

Time to cook: 0 minutes

Approximately 6 servings

Ingredients:

- a teaspoon of vanilla extract
- 3 cups Greek yogurt (low-fat)
- ¼ cup shelled toasted unsalted pistachios 4 tablespoons raw honey
- 28 slices of clementine

Directions:

- Combine the vanilla essence and Greek yogurt in a mixing dish. Fill four tiny parfait glasses with a quarter cup of the mixture.

- Half a spoonful of nuts, half a teaspoon of honey, and five Clementine slices go into each of the four cups.

- Topping the parfait cups with the remaining yogurt mixture, half tablespoon nuts, Clementine segments, and half teaspoon honey Serve right away.

Prosciutto-wrapped Quiche

15 minutes to prepare.

Approximately 8 servings

Ingredients:

- 4 half slices prosciutto 2 beaten egg whites
- 1 egg 1/2 teaspoon rosemary, fresh and chopped, plus a little for garnish 3 tablespoons Greek yoghurt (low fat)
- 1 tablespoon black olives, chopped
- a pinch of freshly ground black pepper salt to taste

Directions:

- Preheat the oven to 400 degrees F and brush a muffin pan with cooking spray.
- Place each prosciutto slice into one of the tray's eight cups.
- Whisk the egg whites and the egg together in a medium mixing basin until smooth. Continue mixing in the

yogurt, rosemary, olives, pepper, and salt.

- Bake until the prosciutto cups are cooked through and the filling is evenly distributed (about 15 minutes).
- Make a rosemary garnish.

Couscous for breakfast.

Time to cook: 25 minutes

Approximately 4 servings

Ingredients:

- 3 quarts of soy milk 1 stick cinnamon
- 4 tsp. sun butter, melted and split 6 tsp. brown sugar, divided 1 pinch salt 1 cup whole-wheat couscous, uncooked quarter cup currants, dried half cup apricots, dried

Directions:

- Pour soy milk and the cinnamon stick into a saucepan over medium heat.
- Allow it to heat for 3 minutes, or until little bubbles appear on the inside of the pan; do not allow it to boil.
- Take the skillet off the heat and add the couscous, currants, apricots, salt, and 4 tablespoons of sugar.
- Cover the pan and let it aside for 20 minutes. Remove the cinnamon stick and discard.
- Toss the couscous with half a teaspoon of sugar and 1 teaspoon melted sun butter in four bowls.
- Serve immediately.

Omelet verde

Time to prepare: 10 minutes

Approximately 4 servings

Ingredients:

- 8 eggs
- 1 finely sliced yellow onion 1 garlic clove, minced
- 1 medium collard greens bunch 3 tablespoons chopped parsley
- 1 tablespoon allspice
- extra virgin olive oil, 5 tbsp
- half a cup grated Parmigiano-Reggiano

Optional: 1 pinch of salt

Directions:

- In a large mixing basin, whisk together the eggs, onion, garlic, collard greens, parsley, and spices.
- Continually pound until all of the Mix the ingredients well.
- Heat the olive oil in a nonstick skillet over medium heat until it is hot.
- Cook for approximately 5 minutes, or until golden brown, after adding the contents of the bowl.
- Flip the omelet with a spatula and cook the second side for 5 minutes or until golden brown.
- Serve on a platter, chop into appropriate amounts, and top with grated cheese before serving.

Quinoa grain.

15 minutes to prepare.

Approximately 4 servings

Ingredients:

- 1 cup almonds 1 teaspoon cinnamon powder 1 quinoa cup 1 cup milk
- 1 teaspoon salt 2 tablespoons honey
- 5 finely chopped dried apricots
- 2 finely chopped dried, pitted dates a teaspoon of vanilla extract

Directions:

- To get a nice nutty taste, roast the almonds in a pan for five minutes or until golden brown.
- Heat the quinoa and cinnamon in a skillet over medium heat until warmed through.
- After that, add the milk and salt, stirring constantly.
- Reduce the heat to low, cover the pot, and let the mixture to simmer for 15 minutes.
- In a saucepan, combine the honey, apricots, dates, vanilla essence, and half of the almonds.
- Top with the remaining almonds and serve in dishes.

Energizing Protein Bars for Breakfast

Time to prepare: 35 minutes.

Approximately 6 servings

Ingredients:

- quarter cup chopped pecans 2 tablespoons chopped pistachios quarter cup ground flaxseeds 1 tablespoon spelt flakes
- dried cherries, ½ cup 1 teaspoon salt
- a half-cup of honey
- 2 tbsp olive oil (extra virgin)
- half teaspoon vanilla essence, quarter cup peanut butter

Directions:

- Start by preheating your oven to 325°F and lightly oiling your baking pan.
- Brush the baking pan with oil after lining it with parchment paper.
- In a mixing dish, combine the nuts, pistachios, flaxseeds, spelt, cherries, and salt.
- Pour the honey, oil, peanut butter, and vanilla extract into a saucepan over medium heat and whisk until the mixture melts.
- Add this to the dry ingredients bowl. and combine well. Smooth the top of the mixture into the prepared baking pan.
- Bake until golden brown and the sides of the pan peel away from the edges.
- On a cutting board, remove the baked bar from the pan and cut it into smaller pieces.

- Store in an airtight jar lined with parchment paper after cooling.
- The bars will keep for up to a week.

Fruity and Nut Muesli

1 hour to prepare

Approximately 2 servings

Ingredients:

- 13 cup chopped almonds 34 cup toasted oats half cup low-fat milk
- half-cup Greek yogurt (low-fat)
- 2 tbsp. raw honey half a green apple, diced

Directions:

- Preheat oven to 350 degrees Fahrenheit. Place the almonds on a baking sheet and bake for 10 minutes, or until golden brown.
- In a mixing dish, combine the toasted oats, milk, and yogurt after cooling.
- Refrigerate for one hour, or until the oats are soft.
- Divide the muesli amongst two bowls, then top with the apple and honey.

Scrambled Eggs with Veggies

15 minutes to cook

Approximately 2 servings

Ingredients:

- 2 tablespoons extra virgin olive oil ½ cup frozen corn kernels 1 medium orange bell pepper, chopped 1 thinly sliced scallion 1/4 teaspoon cumin, freshly ground quarter teaspoon allspice, plus a sprinkle 2 eggs
- 2 beaten egg whites 1 teaspoon cinnamon
- 13 cup shredded white cheddar ½ cup fresh salsa 1 medium avocado, diced
- 2 warmed whole-wheat flour tortillas

Directions:

- In a nonstick pan, heat a teaspoon of olive oil over medium heat.
- Toss and flip the bell pepper for 5 minutes, or until tender; add the corn, scallion, cumin, and allspice and cook for another 3 minutes, or until the scallion wilts.
- Place the mixture on a platter and cover with foil. Set the pan aside after wiping it clean with a paper towel.
- In a mixing dish, whisk together the eggs and egg whites with 2 teaspoons of water, a sprinkle of allspice, and a pinch of cinnamon.
- In the same pan, heat the remaining olive oil over medium heat and add the egg mixture.
- Cook for 30 seconds or until the bottom settles, then stir carefully. Continue stirring for another 2 minutes, then add the shredded cheese and foil-wrapped veggies.
- Avocado, salsa, and tortillas are served on the side.

Chapter Four
Salad Recipes

Mediterranean Salad with Grilled Tofu

15 minutes to prepare.

Approximately 4 servings

Ingredients:

- 1 tablespoon extra virgin olive oil
- lemon juice, quarter cup
- 1 teaspoon oregano cloves, dried half teaspoon salt, chopped garlic
- pepper, freshly ground
- Water-packed 14 ounces tofu extra-firm
- Mediterranean Salad Chopped
- 2 tbsp olive oil (extra virgin)
- cup sliced seedless cucumber quarter cup coarsely chopped Kalamata olives quarter cup chopped scallions 2 medium diced tomatoes 1/4 cup chopped fresh parsley 1 tablespoon wine vinegar quarter teaspoon salt freshly ground pepper

Directions:

- Warm up your grill.
- Combine extra virgin olive oil, lemon juice, oregano, garlic, sea salt, and black pepper in a small bowl; set aside two tablespoons for basting.

- Drain and rinse tofu, then pat dry with paper towels. Cut tofu into 8 half-inch thick slices crosswise and place in a glass dish.
- Turn the tofu to coat it in the lemon juice marinade. Refrigerate for at least 30 minutes after marinating.
- Prepare the salad in the meanwhile.
- Combine all of the salad ingredients in a medium mixing basin. Toss lightly to combine the ingredients.
- Place aside.
- Brush some oil on the grill rack. Drain and discard the marinade from the tofu.
- Grill tofu for 4 minutes each side over medium heat, basting often with the remaining lemon juice marinade.
- Serve the grilled tofu with the salad on the side.

Salad with Mediterranean Barley.

30 minutes to prepare.

Approximately 6 servings

- Ingredients:
- a half-cup of water 1 pound of barley
- 4 tablespoons extra virgin olive oil 2 garlic cloves
- 7 tomatoes, sun-dried
- a tablespoon of balsamic vinegar
- half a cup black olives, chopped
- half cup cilantro, finely chopped

Directions:

- In a saucepan, combine the water and barley; bring to a boil over high heat.
- Reduce the heat to medium-low and cook, covered, for approximately 30 minutes, or until the potatoes are cooked but still firm in the middle.
- Drain the cooked barley and place it in a large mixing bowl to cool to room temperature.
- 2 tablespoons extra virgin olive oil, garlic, sun-dried tomatoes, and balsamic vinegar, pureed until smooth in a blender; pour over barley and mix in remaining olive oil, olives, and cilantro.
- Refrigerate until completely cooled, covered. Before serving, stir everything together well.

Salad with Mediterranean Quinoa.

Time to prepare: 20 minutes

Approximately 4 servings

Ingredients:

- 2 cups water cubes chicken bouillon Ingredients: garlic clove, crushed 1 cup quinoa, uncooked
- half a cup Kalamata olives, chopped 1 big sliced red onion
- 2 cooked big chicken breasts, diced 1 big chopped green bell pepper
- quarter cup chopped fresh chives half cup crumbled feta cheese

- a quarter cup of fresh parsley, chopped
- quarter cup extra virgin olive oil half teaspoon salt a tablespoon of balsamic vinegar
- 2/3 cup freshly squeezed lemon juice

Directions:

- In a saucepan, combine the garlic clove, water, and bouillon cubes; bring to a moderate boil over medium-low heat.
- Cook, covered, for approximately 20 minutes, or until the water has been absorbed and the quinoa is soft.
- Remove the garlic clove and place the cooked quinoa in a large mixing basin. Combine the olives, onion, chicken, bell pepper, feta cheese, chives, parsley, sea salt, extra virgin olive oil, balsamic vinegar, and lemon juice in a large mixing bowl.
- Warm or cooled is fine.

Greek salad.

Time to cook: 0 minutes

Approximately 6 servings

Ingredients:

- tiny red onion, peeled and sliced cucumbers 4 tsp. freshly squeezed lemon juice 3 big ripe tomatoes, diced
- extra virgin olive oil, quarter cup 1 teaspoon dried oregano
- Sea salt
- black pepper, ground

- 6 black Greek olives, pitted and sliced 1 cup feta cheese, crumbled

Directions:

- In a shallow salad dish, combine the onion, cucumber, and tomatoes; season with lemon juice, extra virgin olive oil, oregano, sea salt, and black pepper.
- Serve the salad immediately with the olives and feta cheese.

Salad with almonds, mint, and Kashi.

1 hour to prepare.

Approximately 4 servings

Ingredients:

- 4 tablespoons extra virgin olive oil, divided, with a little more for drizzling 1 finely chopped tiny onion
- to taste with sea salt
- to taste freshly ground black pepper 2 quarts of water
- 1 cup whole grain Kashi Pilaf 2 bay leaves (optional)
- 3 tablespoons lemon juice
- 5 tbsp. natural almond slices, split ¼ cup chopped parsley 8 cherry tomatoes, quartered
- 1/4 cup fresh mint, chopped 4 romaine lettuce leaves

Directions:

- In a large saucepan over medium heat, heat 2 tablespoons extra virgin olive oil.

- Cook, turning periodically, for approximately 5 minutes or until onion is lightly caramelized and soft, adding salt and pepper as needed.

- 2 cups water, Kashi, bay leaves, sea salt, and pepper; bring to a boil, then reduce to a low heat and cook, covered, for approximately 40 minutes or until Kashi is soft.

- Remove bay leaves and transfer to a large mixing bowl, then toss in the remaining extra virgin olive oil and lemon juice.

- Allow to cool to room temperature for at least 20 minutes. Season to taste, then add 4 tablespoons almonds, tomatoes, parsley, and mint, tossing well to combine.

- Place one romaine leaf on each of the four plates and ladle the mixture into the middle; drizzle with extra virgin olive oil and scatter the remaining almonds on top.

Salad with chickpeas

Time to prepare: 40 minutes.

Approximately 6 servings

Ingredients:

- 1 1/2 cups soaked dry chickpeas (reserve liquid) 1 tsp. extra virgin olive oil, chopped garlic clove, 1 quarter teaspoon sea salt sherry vinegar, 3 tbsp
- 16 whole black peppercorns, crushed
- 34 teaspoon oregano, dry
- 3 scallions, half-inch thick slices

- 2 carrots, cut into half-inch dice (4 ounces) 1 cup green bell pepper, chopped
- half a peeled and chopped English cucumber 2 cups cherry tomatoes, halved
- 1 tablespoon basil, shredded
- 1 tablespoon fresh parsley, chopped

Directions:

- In a large saucepan, combine the chickpeas and soaking liquid and season with 34 tablespoons of sea salt.
- Over medium heat, bring the mixture to a moderate boil. Reduce to a low heat and cook for approximately 40 minutes, stirring periodically, or until the chickpeas are soft; drain and add to a large mixing bowl.
- Meanwhile, create the dressing by mashing together the garlic and salt into a paste; transfer to a separate bowl and whisk in the extra virgin olive oil, vinegar, peppercorns, and oregano.
- Allow at least 30 minutes for the garlic dressing to soak into the chickpeas, stirring once.
- Scallions, carrots, bell pepper, cucumber, tomatoes, basil, and parsley are added to the mix.
- Serve.

Salad on Italian bread.

5 minutes to prepare

Approximately 4 servings

Ingredients:

- 3 tbsp lemon juice, freshly squeezed 2 tbsp olive oil (extra virgin)
- Sea salt
- pepper, freshly ground
- 1 halved and sliced red onion
- 1 fennel bulb, cut after removing the stems 1 English cucumber, peeled and sliced
- 1/2 pound tomatoes, diced
- 13 cup halves pitted Kalamata olives 4 slices country bread (whole wheat)
- 1 peeled and halved garlic clove
- 4 oz. ricotta salata cheese, shaved
- basil leaves, half a cup

Directions:

- In a large mixing bowl, combine the lemon juice and extra virgin olive oil; season with sea salt and black pepper.
- Mix in the onion, fennel, cucumber, tomatoes, and olives; toss well and chill for 2 hours.
- When ready, preheat the broiler to 4 inches from the heat source and toast the bread on a baking pan for 2 minutes each side or until nicely browned.
- Rub the toasted bread with the sliced garlic and cut it into 2-inch pieces on a work surface.
- To serve, divide the bread among four shallow dishes and top with the tomato salad, cheese, and basil.

Salad with bulgur.

Time to prepare: 20 minutes

Approximately 4 servings

Ingredients:

- 2 tablespoons unsalted butter
- divided tbsp extra virgin olive oil 2 cups bulgur wheat
- 4 quarts of water
- a quarter teaspoon of salt
- 1 medium cucumber, deseeded and sliced 1/4 cup dill 1 handful pitted and chopped black olives 2 tablespoons red wine vinegar

Directions:

- 1 tablespoon butter and 1 tablespoon olive oil in a saucepan over medium heat
- In the oil, toast the bulgur until it becomes golden brown and crackles.
- Season with salt and 4 cups of water in the pot.
- Cover the pot and cook for approximately 20 minutes, or until all of the water has been absorbed.
- Combine the cucumber, dill, olives, red wine vinegar, and the remaining olive oil in a mixing dish.
- Serve on top of bulgur.

Salad Greek

Time to cook: 0 minutes

Approximately 4 servings

Ingredients:

- 1 lemon's juice
- extra virgin olive oil, 6 tbsp 1 tsp. oregano, dry, black pepper to taste
- 1 red bell pepper, chopped 1 green bell pepper, chopped 1 cucumber, sliced tomatoes, chopped 1 cup feta cheese, crumbled 1 red onion, thinly sliced 1 can black olives, pitted

Directions:

- In a small bowl, whisk together the lemon juice, olive oil, pepper, and oregano.
- Combine the lettuce, bell peppers, cucumber, tomatoes, cheese, and onion in a large mixing basin.
- Toss the salad in this bowl with the salad dressing until it is equally covered, then serve.

Salad of potatoes

Time to cook: 14 minutes

Approximately 4 servings

Ingredients:

- 5 medium peeled and sliced potatoes ¼ onion, coarse salt to taste
- 3 tablespoons mustard 2 cups mayonnaise 1 teaspoon sweet paprika finely sliced Tabasco scallions

Directions:

- Fill a saucepan halfway with water and set it over medium heat.

- Season with coarse salt and cook for about 10 minutes, or until the potatoes are soft.

- Drain the water and dry them out in the saucepan over high heat. Allow the potatoes to cool to room temperature before serving.

- In a mixing dish, grate the onion and combine it with the mustard, mayonnaise, paprika, and spicy sauce.

- Toss the potatoes in the basin so they are equally covered. Top with chopped scallions and divide among four dishes.

Salad of Mediterranean Greens

Time to prepare: 10 minutes

Approximately 4 servings

Ingredients:

- rustic sourdough bread, half loaf
- paprika, quarter teaspoon
- 2 tablespoons coarsely grated manchego
- 7 tablespoons extra virgin olive oil 1 tablespoon sherry vinegar
- a half teaspoon of salt
- 1 teaspoon black pepper, freshly ground 1 teaspoon mustard
- 5 cups young greens, mixed

- 12 thin slices of Serrano ham, finely chopped 34 cup green olives, pitted and halved

Directions:

- Set aside the bread, which has been cut into bite-sized pieces. Preheat oven to 400 degrees Fahrenheit.
- Combine paprika, manchego, and 6 tablespoons olive oil in a mixing basin.
- Toss in the bread cubes until they are uniformly covered in the flavored oil.
- Place the bread on a baking sheet and bake for 8 minutes, or until golden brown. Remove the bread from the oven and cool.
- Combine the vinegar, salt, pepper, mustard, and the remaining olive oil in a separate bowl.
- Toss this mixture with the greens in a larger mixing bowl until they are gently covered with the vinaigrette.
- Toss in the remaining ingredients, including the croutons. Place the salad on four plates and serve.
- This salad has a fantastic flavor and will keep you energetic for the rest of the day.

Salad de lentils

Time to prepare: 10 minutes

Approximately 4 servings

Ingredients:

- extra virgin olive oil, 1 tablespoon 1 1/2 cups leeks, finely sliced 2 teaspoon mustard (whole grain) sherry vinegar, 2 tbsp

- 2 cups lentils, cooked
- 12 cup red grapes, halved, 1/4 cup chopped roasted pistachios
- ¼ cup feta cheese, crumbled
- 3 tablespoons parsley, finely chopped 3 tbsp. mint, coarsely chopped

Directions:

- Heat the extra virgin olive oil in a pan over medium heat; add the leeks and cook, turning occasionally, for approximately 9 minutes, or until transparent and tender. Turn off the heat and add the mustard and sherry vinegar.
- Combine the leek combination, lentils, grapes, pistachios, mint, parsley, sea salt, and pepper in a large mixing basin.
- Enjoy with feta cheese on top!

Chapter Five
Soup and Stews

Soup with Parsley.

15 minutes to prepare.

Approximately 4 to 6 servings

Ingredients:

- 1 tablespoon olive oil 1 bunch fresh flat-leaf parsley, stems cut, parsley leaves set aside for garnish
- 3 big or medium leeks, cut light green and white sections 4 quarts water
- 4 cups water or 4 cups low-sodium vegetable or chicken broth
- 4 green onions, chopped (approximately 3-inch green and white sections) 1 medium zucchini, peeled and shredded using a grater
- 2 tsp. salt

Directions:

- In a large stockpot placed over medium high heat, pour in the oil.
- Cook, stirring constantly, for approximately 5 minutes, or until the leeks turn light in color.
- Bring the mixture to a boil with the broth or water, green onions, and zucchini.
- Reduce the heat to medium-low and cook for approximately 10 minutes. Remove the soup from the heat and

set it aside to cool for approximately 10 minutes. Garnish with parsley leaves and serve warm.

Delicious Lentil Soup

1 hour to prepare.

Approximately 4 servings

Ingredients:

- 1 1/2 cups lentils (brown)
- ¼ cup extra virgin olive oil
- 2 garlic cloves, squeezed 1 big onion, diced 1 sliced carrot 1/4 teaspoon dried oregano 1/4 teaspoon dry rosemary 2 dried bay leaves
- 1 tablespoon of tomato paste
- 1 tablespoon of red wine vinegar

Directions:

- Fill a big pot halfway with water and add the lentils.
- Bring to a boil over medium heat; simmer for 10–20 minutes and drain in a sieve.
- Clean the pot, then add the olive oil and heat on medium.
- Simmer until the onions and garlic are tender, then add the carrots and cook for an additional 5 minutes.
- Add the lentils, 1 1/2 cups water, oregano, rosemary, and bay leaves to the pot.

- Reduce the heat to low and cook for 10 minutes after the pan comes to a boil.
- Add the tomato paste and continue to cook for another 30 minutes, stirring occasionally.
- Add water until the soup reaches the desired consistency. To taste, drizzle with vinegar.

Barley Soup with Veggies

1 hour 30 minutes to cook

Approximately 4 servings

Ingredients:

- 1 cup barley 2 quarts vegetable broth 2 celery stalks, diced 2 big carrots, chopped
- 1 can (15 ounces) drained garbanzo beans 1 (14.5 ounce) can tomatoes with liquid 1 zucchini, chopped 1 chopped onion
- three bay leaves
- 1 teaspoon parsley, dry 1 teaspoon of white sugar
- a teaspoon of garlic powder
- 1 teaspoon Worcestershire 1 tablespoon paprika
- a teaspoon of curry powder
- half teaspoon black pepper, ground 1 teaspoon salt

Directions:

- In a large soup pot over medium heat, add the stock.

- Celery, carrots, barley, garbanzo beans, zucchini, tomatoes, onion, bay leaves, parsley, sugar, garlic powder, Worcestershire sauce, paprika, curry powder, sea salt, and pepper are added to the pot.

- Bring to a moderate boil, then cover and reduce to medium low heat.

- Cook until the soup is thick, approximately 90 minutes. Remove bay leaves and serve immediately.

Soup with chickpeas

30 minutes to prepare.

Approximately 6 servings

Ingredients:

- 1 tablespoon olive oil (extra virgin) quarter cup freshly squeezed lemon juice 4 garlic cloves, chopped cup sliced onion (15-oz.) chickpeas, washed and drained

- half a cup parsley, chopped 1 bay leaf, 1/2 teaspoon salt Spice Oil from Morocco

Directions:

- In a medium saucepan placed over medium heat, heat extra virgin olive oil; add garlic and onion and cook, stirring occasionally, for approximately 10 minutes, or until they begin to brown.

- 4 cups water, chickpeas, parsley, and bay leaf; whisk and cover and cook to a medium boil.

- Reduce heat to low and cook for 15 minutes. Remove the bay leaf and add the sea salt.
- In a food processor, blend the soup in batches until extremely smooth and creamy.
- Return the pureed soup to the pan and add the lemon juice to taste.
- Pour the soup into dishes and top with a half teaspoon Moroccan Spice Oil and chopped parsley.
- Enjoy!

Soup with Red Lentil Beans

45 minutes to prepare.

Approximately 4 servings

Ingredients:

- 2 tbsp extra virgin olive oil, plus more for drizzling Ingredients: cup dry red lentil beans, washed 2 finely sliced carrots - 2 big diced onions 8 quarts chicken broth
- diced ripe tomatoes 1 teaspoon cumin powder Sea salt
- peppercorns
- 2 cups spinach, fresh

Directions:

- Lentils should be soaked for at least 2 hours.
- Boil the lentils in a saucepan over medium high heat until nearly done.

- Heat extra virgin olive oil in a soup pot over medium heat; add chopped onions and carrots and cook for 4 minutes, or until soft.

- Simmer for approximately 40 minutes, or until lentils are soft, with stock, tomatoes, cumin, sea salt, and pepper.

- Just before serving, stir in the spinach until it has wilted somewhat and sprinkle with extra virgin olive oil.

Soup made with chickpeas and lentil beans.

1 hour to prepare.

Approximately 4 servings

Ingredients:

- 2 tbsp olive oil (extra virgin) 2 big diced onions
- 2 garlic cloves, minced
- 4 big chopped celery stalks 1 cup washed dried lentils 6 quarts of water
- fresh ginger, grated half teaspoon
- 1/2 teaspoon cinnamon
- 34 teaspoon turmeric 1 teaspoon cumin salt, to taste (16-ounce) washed chickpeas in can 3 cubed ripe tomatoes
- half lemon, finely sliced half lemon juice half cup chopped cilantro or parsley

Directions:

- Heat extra virgin olive oil in a soup pot; add onions and sauté for 5 minutes, or until aromatic and soft.

- Add the garlic and celery and cook for another 3 minutes, or until the onions are golden.

- Bring the lentils, 6 cups water, and spices to a moderate boil over medium high heat; reduce to medium-low heat and cook for approximately 40 minutes, or until the lentils are cooked.

- If necessary, add chickpeas, tomatoes, and additional water and seasonings. Continue to cook for another 15 minutes.

- Pour the soup into a serving basin and stir with the freshly squeezed lemon juice, cilantro, or parsley.

- Serve immediately with 1 or 2 lemon slices on top of each dish.

Rotelle Soup with Fish

30 minutes to prepare.

Approximately 4 servings

Ingredients:

- 1 tablespoon extra virgin olive oil plus more for drizzling 1 teaspoon garlic, minced
- half a can crushed tomatoes 1 onion, chopped 1 rotelle pasta cup
- rosemary, quarter teaspoon
- shells of a dozen mussels Monkfish, 1 pound

Directions:

- Heat extra virgin olive oil in a saucepan over medium heat; add garlic and onion and cook for 4 minutes or until tender.

- Season with sea salt and pepper and simmer for approximately 15 minutes after adding the tomatoes, water, pasta, and rosemary.

- Clean the mussels and chop the monkfish into tiny pieces; add to the broth and continue to cook for another 10 minutes, or until all of the mussel shells have opened.

- Remove the closed shells and serve the soup with crusty bread and additional extra virgin olive oil poured on top.

Soup with beans and cabbage.

Time to prepare: 50 minutes.

Approximately 6 servings

Ingredients:

- ¼ cup extra virgin olive oil
- 2 carrots, diced half cup chopped onion celery stalks
- 14.5-ounce diced tomatoes can
- a quarter teaspoon of dried sage 6 parsley sprigs
- 1 bay leaf
- 8 quarts of water
- ½ pound diced baked ham 1 (14.5-ounce) cannellini beans, drained

- 6 cups green cabbage, chopped 1/2 pound Yukon potatoes, diced
- ¼ cup polenta (instant) Black pepper with salt

Directions:

- Heat extra virgin olive oil in a large stock pot over medium heat until heated; add onions, celery, and carrots and sauté for approximately 7 minutes, or until onions are translucent.
- Reduce heat to low and simmer for approximately 10 minutes after adding the tomatoes, sage, parsley, and bay leaf.
- Over medium high heat, stir in the water and bring to a rolling boil.
- Reduce heat to medium-low and stir in the beans, ham, cabbage, and potatoes.
- Cook until potatoes are cooked, approximately 20 minutes.
- Stir in the polenta and cook for 5 minutes, seasoning with salt and pepper.
- Immediately ladle the soup into bowls and serve.

Soup de Minestrone

Time to cook: 8 hours

Approximately 8 servings

Ingredients:

- 3 celery stalks, cut carrots, cleaned, sliced Italian chicken sausage links, sliced 4 cups chicken stock 1 onion, chopped (28-ounce) can diced tomatoes (14.5-ounce) cans navy beans, rinsed

- 3 sliced zucchinis 1 cup orzo Sea salt
- parmesan cheese, grated 1/2 teaspoon sage bay leaves, dried
- 2 thyme sprigs Sea salt

Directions:

- Stir together onions, tomatoes, beans, celery, carrots, sausage, stock, sage, thyme, and bay leaves in a 5-quart slow cooker over low heat; simmer for approximately 8 hours.
- During the final 30 minutes of cooking, add the zucchini and orzo. Season with salt and pepper, then divide the soup among 8 bowls, remove the bay leaves, and top with a tablespoon of grated Parmesan cheese on each dish.
- Enjoy!

Soup with spicy lentils and spinach.

30 minutes to prepare.

Approximately 4 to 6 servings

Ingredients:

- 2 tbsp olive oil (extra virgin)
- neatly sliced huge yellow onion 1 big minced garlic clove 1 teaspoon dried mint flakes
- 1/2 teaspoon crushed red pepper 14 teaspoon sumac

- 14 teaspoon cumin 14 teaspoon coriander Sea salt
- peppercorns 1 teaspoon of sugar 1 tablespoon flour 1 cup water, plus more if necessary
- 6 cups vegetable broth (low sodium) 1/2 cup washed tiny brown lentils
- 10-12 oz. chopped leaf spinach, frozen (no need to thaw) 2 cups parsley, chopped
- lime juice, 2 tbsp

Directions:

- In a big ceramic saucepan, heat 2 tablespoons extra virgin olive oil over medium heat.
- Add the chopped onions and cook for 4 minutes, or until golden brown.
- Cook for approximately 2 minutes, stirring regularly, with the garlic, dried mint, all spices, sugar, and flour.
- Bring the water and broth to a boil over medium high heat, then add the lentils and spinach and simmer for approximately 5 minutes.
- Reduce the heat to low and simmer, covered, for approximately 20 minutes, or until the lentils are cooked.
- Remove the pot from the heat and stir in the chopped parsley and lime juice; let aside for at least 5 minutes to allow flavors to blend before serving with your favorite rustic Italian bread or pita bread.

Tomato Pesto Soup with Three Beans

30 minutes to prepare.

Approximately 6 servings

Ingredients:

- Pesto Sauce with Tomatoes
- 4-6 cloves garlic
- 1 cup tomatoes, diced 15 basil leaves, big
- extra virgin olive oil, half cup
- a half-cup of grated Parmesan Sea salt
- peppercorns
- Soup 1 tablespoon extra virgin olive oil, plus more for drizzling 1 peeled and chopped russet potato
- 1/2 cup tomatoes, diced
- 8 oz. chopped French green beans 1 teaspoon paprika
- 1 teaspoon of coriander Sea salt
- white vinegar tbsp. black pepper 6 cups vegetable broth 6 cups red kidney beans, boiled
- 2 cups white kidney beans, cooked
- 13 cup pine nuts, roasted Leaves of basil
- Parmesan cheese, grated

Directions:

- To make tomato pesto sauce, follow these steps:
- In a food processor, mix the garlic and tomatoes until thoroughly incorporated.
- Continue pulsing after adding basil.

- Pulse in extra virgin olive oil in a slow, steady stream until smooth.

- Transfer the pesto to a mixing bowl and add the grated Parmesan cheese; season with salt and pepper to taste and leave aside.

- Heat 2 tablespoons extra virgin olive oil in a heavy saucepan or Dutch oven over medium high heat until hot but not smokey.

- Reduce the heat to medium and add the diced potato. Cook for approximately 4 minutes, stirring periodically.

- Cook, covered, for approximately 4 minutes longer after adding the tomatoes, green beans, spices, and vinegar.

- Remove the cover and increase the heat to medium-high; add the vegetable broth and simmer for 5 minutes.

- Reduce the heat to medium and cover the saucepan once more.

- Cook for 10 minutes before adding the red and white kidney beans.

- Cook for another 5 minutes, or until the beans are thoroughly heated.

- Remove the saucepan from the heat and add the tomato pesto.

- Drizzle extra virgin olive oil, toasted pine nuts, fresh basil leaves, and grated Parmesan cheese over each dish of soup.

- With your favorite Italian bread, serve.

Soup with Lemon.

Time to cook: 23 minutes

Approximately 8 servings

Ingredients:

- 8 cups low-sodium chicken or veggie stock 2 tbsp olive oil (extra virgin)
- flour (quarter cup) 2 tablespoons butter
- 1 cup orzo
- 4 eggs
- 34 cup lemon juice, freshly squeezed quarter teaspoon ground white pepper to taste 8 slices of lemon

Directions:

- Bring stock to a moderate boil in a soup pot over medium heat; decrease heat to a simmer.
- Combine extra virgin olive oil, flour, and butter in a small basin. 2 cups hot stock, whisked into flour mixture until thoroughly blended Stir the flour mixture into the liquid in a slow, steady stream for approximately 10 minutes.
- Cook for another 5 minutes after adding the orzo.
- Meanwhile, in a small mixing bowl, whisk together the eggs and lemon juice until thoroughly combined and frothy.
- Whisk a cup of the heated soup mixture into the egg mixture until well mixed.
- Add the egg mixture to the soup pot and stir well to combine. Cook for 10 minutes, or until the soup has

thickened.

- Season with salt and pepper before ladling into a serving dish. Serve immediately with lemon slices on top.

Beef Stew with Red Wine from the Mediterranean.

Time to cook: 23 minutes

Approximately 8 servings

Ingredients:

- 1 tablespoon olive oil (extra virgin) 1 chopped onion 1/2 cup flour
- a half teaspoon of salt
- 1 teaspoon black pepper, freshly ground
- pound slices of beef shoulder, chopped into little pieces 2 garlic cloves
- 2 cups halved crimini mushrooms 2 sliced medium carrots 2 chopped celery stalks 1 cup parsley, chopped
- 1 can chopped tomatoes, 14 oz 1 teaspoon oregano, dry
- cups of granulated sugar beef stock with minimal sodium 2 thyme sprigs bay leaf cup red wine

Directions:

- In a Dutch oven, heat extra virgin olive oil over medium high heat until heated but not smoky.
- Stir in the onions and cook for 5 minutes, or until they are gently browned. Place the onions on a platter and put

them aside.

- Meanwhile, in a large mixing bowl, combine flour, sea salt, and black pepper; dredge meat in the flour mixture.

- Shake off any excess flour before adding the meat to the pan; cook for 5 minutes each side or until both sides are browned.

- Return the onions, garlic, mushrooms, carrots, celery, oregano, thyme, and bay leaf to the pan.

- Stir in the stock, tomatoes, wine, and sugar until everything is completely combined. Bring the mixture to a low boil and then turn off the heat. Cook until the beef is soft, approximately 3 hours.

- Before serving, stir in the minced parsley.

- For a delicious supper, serve over mashed potatoes, polenta, or orzo.

Chickpeas with Plum Tomatoes Chicken Stew

1 hour 15 minutes to cook

Approximately 6 servings

Ingredients:

- 2 tbsp olive oil (extra virgin) 4 chicken thighs, skinless
- 1 drained 14-ounce can chickpeas 1 sliced celery stalk
- 1 teaspoon turmeric, half teaspoon ginger, half teaspoon cinnamon, quarter teaspoon sea salt

- 1 teaspoon black pepper, freshly ground 1 plum tomato 28-ounce can
- quarter cup red lentils half cup long-grain rice
- 6 cups chicken stock (low sodium)
- quarter cup lemon juice, freshly squeezed 1 onion, chopped half cup cilantro, chopped

Directions:

- In a stockpot, heat extra virgin olive oil over medium high heat.
- Cook for 3 minutes each side, or until chicken is lightly browned.
- Cook for approximately 3 minutes, or until the onion, chickpeas, celery, and spices are cooked through.
- Bring the tomatoes, rice, lentils, and stock to a slow boil, stirring occasionally.
- Reduce to a low heat and cook, covered, for 15 minutes or until lentils are cooked. Stir in lemon juice.
- To serve, divide the stew among six bowls and top each with 2 tablespoons chopped cilantro.

Soup with Italian potatoes and leeks.

Time to cook: 43 minutes

Approximately 6 servings

Ingredients:

- 2 tbsp olive oil (extra virgin) 1 tablespoon butter

- 1 medium sweet onion, diced 1 1/2 pounds washed and thinly sliced leeks 1 cup white wine, dry
- 3 pounds peeled and sliced potatoes 6 cups chicken stock (low sodium)
- half-cup heavy cream to taste with sea salt
- to taste white pepper

Directions:

- In a large stockpot, heat extra virgin olive oil and butter over medium high heat until butter is melted and frothy.
- Sauté for approximately 10 minutes, or until onions and leeks are soft and gently browned. Cook for 5 minutes after adding the wine.
- Stir in the potatoes and stock, then boil for approximately 25 minutes, or until the potatoes are tender.
- Blend the contents in a blender until it is smooth and creamy.
- Return the soup to the pot and stir in the cream; cook for 3 minutes, then season with salt and pepper.
- Serve right away.

Soup with chicken

Time to prepare: 40 minutes Approximately 8 servings

Ingredients:

- 1 pound chopped skinless, boneless chicken breasts 1 teaspoon of black pepper
- a tablespoon of Greek seasoning

- extra virgin olive oil, 1 tablespoon 1 minced garlic clove
- ¼ cup white wine 4 finely chopped green onions
- 7 cups chicken broth (low sodium) 1 tablespoon capers, drained 1/4 cup pitted and sliced Greek olives 1/4 cup chopped sun-dried tomatoes 1 1/2 cups orzo pasta /2 teaspoon oregano, minced 1 1/2 teaspoon basil, minced
- 1 tsp. fresh parsley, minced 2 tablespoons lemon juice

Directions:

- Season the chicken with salt, pepper, and Greek spice.
- Heat extra virgin olive oil in a Dutch oven over medium high heat until hot but not smokey.
- Cook for approximately 10 minutes, or until the chicken is no longer pink; transfer to a platter and set aside.
- Stir in the chicken, broth, capers, olives, tomatoes, oregano, and basil and cook for 1 minute, or until aromatic.
- Reduce heat to low and cover for approximately 15 minutes.
- Bring the sauce to a boil, then add the orzo and simmer for another 10 minutes, or until the pasta is cooked.
- Serve immediately with parsley and lemon juice.

Soup with Tuscan vegetables.

15 minutes to prepare.

Approximately 6 servings

Ingredients:

- 1 can (15 ounces) washed and split cannellini beans 1 tablespoon olive oil (extra virgin)
- 1 cup onion, chopped
- tsp. chopped sage leaves 1 garlic clove, minced half cup diced celery half cup diced carrot half cups diced zucchini
- 1 tablespoon thyme leaves, chopped
- quarter teaspoon black pepper half teaspoon sea salt
- 1 can chopped tomatoes (14.5 oz) 32 ounces chicken broth with minimal sodium 2 cups baby spinach, chopped
- 13 cup parmesan cheese, grated

Directions:

- In a small dish, mash half of the beans and put aside.
- Heat extra virgin olive oil in a large soup pot over medium high heat, then add onion, garlic, celery, carrots, zucchini, sage, thyme, sea salt, and pepper.
- Cook for approximately 5 minutes, or until the veggies are soft, stirring periodically.
- Bring to a boil with the tomatoes and broth.
- Cook for another 3 minutes, or until the spinach is wilted, after adding the mashed, whole beans, and spinach.

- Serve immediately by ladling the soup into dishes and topping with Parmesan cheese.

Soup with Roasted Veggies

Time to prepare: 40 minutes.

Approximately 4 servings

Ingredients:

- 350 g potatoes, diced half tsp. chopped rosemary 5 garlic cloves tbsp. extra virgin olive oil green and yellow bell peppers, diced 1 half cup carrot juice 1 big red onion, diced 1 yellow zucchini, chopped
- 12 tsp. minced rosemary 370 g diced Italian tomatoes
- 1 teaspoon tarragon, fresh

Directions:

- Preheat the oven to 4500 degrees Fahrenheit.
- Combine garlic and extra virgin olive oil in a roasting pan and roast for approximately 5 minutes, or until oil begins to crackle.
- Toss in the peppers, potatoes, and rosemary to coat; roast for another 15 minutes or until potatoes are soft and golden.
- Add the onion and yellow zucchini and continue to roast for another 15 minutes, or until the zucchini is soft.
- Bring tomatoes, carrot juice, and tarragon to a boil in a medium saucepan over medium heat.

- Add the roasted veggies to the pan and mix in a small quantity of water, scraping up any browned parts that cling to the pan and adding to the pot.
- Cook for approximately 2 minutes, or until well heated. Serve right away.

Stew of Moroccan Beef

Time to prepare: 20 minutes

Approximately 6 servings

Ingredients:

- 1 34 pound beef tenderloin, chopped 3 tablespoons extra virgin olive oil to taste with sea salt and pepper
- 1 half teaspoon ground cinnamon 2 garlic cloves, chopped 1 big carrot, diced 1 large onion, chopped 2 tsp cumin powder
- paprika (1 tablespoon)
- ½ cup golden raisins 1 15-ounce can garbanzo beans, drained
- half a cup pitted and diced Kalamata olives 2 c. beef stock
- half cup fresh cilantro, chopped 1 teaspoon of lemon zest

Directions:

- 2 tablespoons extra virgin olive oil, heated in a heavy big pot over medium high heat
- Season the meat with salt and pepper to taste.

- Cook for approximately 3 minutes, or until the steak is browned on both sides.
- Place the chicken on a platter and put it aside.
- Cook, turning occasionally, for approximately 10 minutes or until the veggies are soft, adding the remaining oil, garlic, carrot, and onion to the pan.
- After 1 minute, add the garbanzo beans, raisins, olives, broth, and cilantro and bring to a mild boil.
- Reduce heat to low and cook for 5 minutes, or until the juices thicken. Add the meat, along with any liquids that have gathered.
- Serve with a squeeze of lemon zest.

Bean Stew from Tuscany.

2 hours to prepare.

Approximately 6 servings

Ingredients:

- 3 tablespoons extra virgin olive oil 6 cups water cups dried cannellini, cleaned and soaked overnight 2 garlic cloves, quartered piece whole-grain bread, cubed 1 1/2 cup vegetable broth
- 6 sprigs fresh rosemary, chopped 1 tablespoon
- freshly ground black pepper, quarter teaspoon 1 tsp. sea salt 6 garlic cloves, chopped 3 peeled carrots, diced 1 yellow onion, chopped
- 1 bay leaf

Directions:

- To make croutons, follow these steps:
- In a large frying pan set over medium heat, heat 2 tablespoons extra virgin olive oil; add chopped garlic and sauté for approximately 1 minute, or until fragrant.
- Remove the skillet from the heat and allow the garlic soak the oil for at least 10 minutes.
- Return the pan to the heat after discarding the garlic.
- Add the bread cubes to the pan and cook for approximately 5 minutes, or until gently browned, turning often.
- Place the baked bread in a mixing basin and put it aside.
- In a soup saucepan over high heat, combine the water, white beans, bay leaf, and half teaspoon of sea salt; bring to a rolling boil.
- Reduce to a low heat and cook, partly covered, for 75 minutes or until the beans are soft; drain the beans and save half cup of the cooking liquid.
- Bay leaf should be removed and discarded.
- Set aside the beans in a large mixing dish.
- Half cup cooked beans and saved cooking liquid in a separate dish; mash with a fork until smooth.
- Stir the mashed beans into the remaining cooked beans to thoroughly combine them.
- Return to the heat and pour the remaining extra virgin olive oil to the empty saucepan.
- Add the onion and carrots and cook for 7 minutes, or until the carrots are crisp and soft.

- Sauté for approximately 1 minute, or until garlic quarters are aromatic. Bring the bean mixture, stock, rosemary, pepper, and the remaining salt to a moderate boil, then reduce to a low heat.
- Cook for approximately 5 minutes, or until the stew is well heated.
- Pour the stew into bowls and top with croutons; serve with a rosemary sprig on top of each dish.

Cucumber Soup (cold).

Time to cook: 0 minutes

Approximately 4 to 6 servings

Ingredients:

- 1 lemon juice 1/2 cup minced fresh parsley 2 cucumbers, medium
- 1 1/2 cups chicken broth (low sodium) 1 cup plain fat-free yogurt
- a half-cup of fat-free half-and-half
- To taste, season with salt and freshly ground black pepper. fresh dill, chopped

Directions:

- Combine lemon juice, parsley, and cucumbers in a blender or food processor and purée until smooth.
- Half of the puree should be put aside on a dish.
- In a medium-sized mixing bowl, combine yogurt, half-and-half, and broth.

- Puree half of the yogurt mixture into the pureed mixture in the blender until well combined.
- Refrigerate in a jar after seasoning with salt and pepper.
- Using the leftover yogurt mixture and puree, repeat the process.
- To serve, stir the soup and top with fresh dill.

Soup with curried cauliflower.

Time to prepare: 20 minutes

Approximately 4 to 6 servings

Ingredients:

- 13 cup cashews, uncooked
- tsp. extra virgin olive oil 34 cup water 1 medium diced onion
- 1 can (14-ounce) coconut milk (light)
- 1 big cauliflower head, cut into little pieces
- a quarter teaspoon of cinnamon powder
- a tablespoon of evaporated cane sugar 1 teaspoon turmeric powder 1 tablespoon curry powder
- quarter cup cilantro, chopped Onions caramelized Salt

Directions:

- In a blender, grind the cashews until they are finely ground.

- Blend the cashews with three-quarters of a cup of water for another two minutes.
- Set aside the mixture after straining it through a fine mesh strainer into a basin.
- In a big saucepan over low heat, pour in the olive oil.
- Cook onions till golden brown in heated olive oil.
- Combine the cashew milk, coconut milk, cauliflower, cinnamon, sugar, turmeric, curry powder, and salt in a large mixing bowl.
- Bring to a slow boil with enough water to cover the mixture.
- Reduce the heat to low and cook for 10 minutes, or until the cauliflower is soft.
- Blend the ingredients in an immersion blender until it reaches the desired consistency.
- Return the pot to the heat.
- Serve the hot soup in bowls with cilantro and onions on the side.

Soup with chicken and lemon.

15 minutes to prepare.

Approximately 4 servings

Ingredients:

- 2 cans reduced-sodium chicken broth (14 half-ounce) ½ cup long-grain white rice 1 tiny sliced carrot 1 garlic clove, coarsely chopped

- quarter cup lemon juice, freshly squeezed
- 1 red bell pepper, carefully sliced into tiny pieces 2 cups cooked and diced chicken breast
- 2 tbsp. fresh basil, minced 1 tbsp. cornstarch can (12 fluid ounce) fat-free evaporated milk, split

Directions:

- Boil the broth in a medium-sized pot.
- Cook, stirring occasionally, for at least 10 minutes, or until rice is soft.
- Combine the garlic, lemon juice, bell pepper, and chicken in a mixing bowl.
- Combine cornstarch and 1 tablespoon evaporated milk in a small dish; whisk the mixture into the soup before gradually adding the remaining milk.
- Bring the liquid to a low boil.
- Remove the soup from the heat and serve with a basil garnish.

Soup with Moroccan vegetables.

45 minutes to prepare.

Approximately 5 servings

Ingredients:

- 1 tablespoon olive oil
- 2 garlic cloves, smashed
- 1 big yellow onion, coarsely chopped 2 tsp cumin powder

- 1 teaspoon coriander powder
- chili powder (quarter teaspoon)
- 500g carrots, peeled and sliced
- 600g sweet potato, peeled and orange 6 cups chicken stock (low sodium) 300g chickpeas, washed and drained half a small lemon, juiced
- to taste with sea salt and pepper Croutons of Turkish bread for serving

Directions:

- Heat olive oil in a saucepan over medium high heat; cook garlic and onions, stirring constantly, for approximately 3 minutes.
- Stir in the cumin, coriander, and chili powder, and simmer, stirring constantly for for 1 minute.
- Cook, stirring occasionally, for approximately 5 minutes after adding the carrots and sweet potato. Add the stock, cover, and bring to a slow boil.
- Reduce the heat to low and cook for approximately 20 minutes, or until the veggies are soft, stirring regularly.
- Stir in the chickpeas, cover, and cook for 10 minutes, or until they soften.
- Blend the soup in stages in a blender until completely smooth. Reheat the soup in the saucepan over medium low heat.
- 1 tablespoon lemon juice, as well as salt and pepper to taste

- Heat the soup for approximately 30 seconds, stirring frequently, or until it is barely warm (do not boil).
- Divide across bowls, top with croutons, and season with salt and pepper.
- Enjoy!

Soup with Italian Beans

30 minutes to prepare.

Approximately 4 servings

Ingredients:

- 1 tablespoon extra virgin olive oil 1 onion, chopped celery stalk, chopped 1 garlic clove, squeezed white kidney beans, rinsed and drained 1 chicken broth can
- quarter teaspoon freshly crushed black pepper 2 cups water 1 sprinkle dried thyme bunch finely sliced fresh spinach 1 tablespoon lemon juice, freshly squeezed Topping: grated Parmesan cheese

Directions:

- In a large saucepan, heat the oil and add the onion and celery. Cook for 8 minutes, or until vegetables are soft.
- Cook for another 30 seconds after adding the garlic.
- Stir in the beans, broth, 2 cups water, pepper, and thyme gradually. Bring to a boil, then lower to a low heat and continue to cook for 15 minutes.

- 2 cups of the bean mixture should be put aside from the soup.
- Blend the remaining soup until smooth, then return it to the pot and toss in the beans that you saved aside.
- Add the spinach and bring to a gentle boil.
- Cook until the spinach has wilted, then add the lemon juice and turn off the heat. Serve on four dishes with grated Parmesan cheese on top.

Stew in the Crockpot

Time to cook: 10 hours

Approximately 10 servings

Ingredients:

- 2 cups diced zucchini, 2 cups cubed eggplant, 1 can tomato sauce
- 1 butternut squash, peeled, seeded, and chopped 1 10oz bag frozen okra, thawed 1 cup minced onion 1 garlic clove chopped half cup vegetable broth 1 carrot, finely sliced 1 tomato, diced 13 cup raisins quarter teaspoon paprika half teaspoon powdered cumin half teaspoon ground turmeric quarter teaspoon ground cinnamon

Directions:

- In a slow cooker, combine all ingredients, cover, and cook on low for 10 hours or until veggies are tender.

Chapter Six Poultry, Seafood and Meat Recipes

Bruschetta with chicken

Time to prepare: 20 minutes

Approximately 4 servings

Ingredients:

- 5ml extra virgin olive oil, split
- 1 chicken breast, boneless and skinless Cherry tomatoes, 80g
- balsamic vinegar, 5 mL 10 g basil leaves, fresh
- 1 small garlic clove, minced 1 small sliced onion

Directions:

- Cook the chicken in half of the oil in a pan over medium heat. Meanwhile, prepare the veggies and chop basil leaves into slivers.
- Sauté the garlic and onion in the remaining oil for approximately 3 minutes. For approximately 5 minutes, stir in the basil and tomatoes.
- Pour in the vinegar.
- Cook until the chicken is well cooked, then serve with the onion and tomato mixture on top.

Chicken with Coconut.

Time to prepare: 10 minutes

Approximately 4 servings

Ingredients:

- 20g shredded coconut 30g almond meal
- 1 teaspoon salt 1 egg, tiny
- 100g boneless, skinless chicken breast
- coconut oil (7.5 mL)

Directions:

- Combine shredded coconut, almond flour, and sea salt in a mixing bowl.
- In a second dish, whisk the egg; dip the chicken in the egg, then roll in the flour mixture until well coated.
- In a medium-sized skillet, heat the coconut oil and cook the chicken until the crust starts to brown.
- Place the chicken in the oven and bake for 10 minutes at 350°F.

Burgers with turkey.

Time to prepare: 10 minutes

Approximately 4 servings

Ingredients:

- 1 big white egg
- 1 cup chopped red onion 34 cup chopped fresh mint 1/2 cup dry bread crumbs 1 teaspoon dried dill
- 13 cup crumbled feta cheese 34 kg ground turkey Spray for cooking

- 4 hamburger buns, toasted and sliced into strips red bell pepper 2 tablespoons lime juice

Directions:

- In a mixing bowl, lightly whisk the egg white, then add the onion, mint, breadcrumbs, dill, cheese, turkey, and lime juice, mixing well after each addition. Divide the turkey mixture into four equal burger patties.
- Cook on medium-high in a large nonstick skillet sprayed with cooking spray.
- Place the patties in the pan with care and cook for 8 minutes on each side, or until done to your liking.
- Place the burgers on the cut buns and garnish with pepper strips after they've been cooked.

Greek Salad with Chicken

Time to cook: 0 minutes

Approximately 4 servings

Ingredients:

- extra virgin olive oil, 1 tablespoon
- 13 cup vinegar (red wine) a teaspoon of garlic powder
- quarter teaspoon of sea salt quarter teaspoon of freshly ground pepper
- half-cup cooked chicken, chopped 6 cups romaine lettuce, chopped
- ½ cup crumbled feta cheese 1 cucumber, peeled, seeded, and diced 2 medium tomatoes, chopped

- half cup ripe black olives, sliced
- half a cup red onion, coarsely chopped

Directions:

- Whisk together extra virgin olive oil, vinegar, garlic powder, dill, sea salt, and pepper in a large mixing basin.
- Toss together the chicken, lettuce, cucumber, tomatoes, feta, and olives. Enjoy!

Chicken Braised with Olives

1 hour 30 minutes to cook

Approximately 4 servings

Ingredients:

- 1 tablespoon olive oil (extra virgin)
- 4 chicken legs, peeled and chopped into drumsticks and thighs 1 cup canned chicken broth with minimal sodium 1 cup dry white wine 4 thyme sprigs 1 tablespoon minced fresh ginger 3/43rd cup chickpeas, drained, washed half cup green olives, pitted and coarsely chopped 2 garlic cloves, minced carrots, diced medium yellow onion, diced
- 13 c. raisins 1 cup of liquid

Directions:

- Preheat the oven to 350 degrees Fahrenheit.
- In a Dutch oven or a large ovenproof skillet, heat extra virgin olive oil over medium heat.
- Add the chicken pieces to the skillet and cook for 5 minutes each side, or until both sides are browned and

crisped.

- Remove the cooked chicken from the pan and place it on a platter.

- Reduce the heat to low and add the garlic, onion, carrots, and ginger to the same skillet; simmer, turning occasionally, for 5 minutes or until the onion is translucent and soft.

- Bring the mixture to a slow boil with the water, chicken broth, and wine.

- Stir in the thyme and return the chicken to the pot. Return the mixture to a boil and cover.

- Place in the oven for approximately 45 minutes to braise.

- Stir in the chickpeas, olives, and raisins after removing the saucepan from the oven.

- Return to the oven and braise for another 20 minutes, uncovered. Take the skillet out of the oven and discard the thyme.

- Serve right away.

Chicken Braised with Mushrooms and Olives

Time to prepare: 35 minutes.

Approximately 4 servings

Ingredients:

- chicken, sliced into half-pound portions Sea salt
- pepper, freshly ground

- 1 tbsp. extra virgin olive oil + 1 tsp. 16 garlic cloves, peeled
- half cup white wine 10 ounces cremini mushrooms, cleaned, trimmed, and halved
- 13 cup chicken stock half cup pitted green olives

Directions:

- Over medium-high heat, heat a large skillet.
- Season the chicken with salt and pepper in the meanwhile.
- In a hot pan, add 1 tablespoon extra virgin olive oil and the chicken, skin side down; cook for 6 minutes or until browned.
- Place on a serving plate and set aside.
- In the same pan, add the remaining 1 teaspoon extra virgin olive oil and sauté the garlic and mushrooms for approximately 6 minutes, or until browned.
- Bring the wine to a mild boil, then decrease the heat and cook for 1 minute.
- Return the chicken to the pan, along with the chicken broth and olives. Return the mixture to a low boil, then lower to a low heat and cover and cook for approximately 20 minutes, or until the chicken is cooked through.

Olives, Mustard Greens, and Lemon Chicken

30 minutes to prepare.

Approximately 6 servings

Ingredients:

- 1 tbsp. freshly squeezed lemon juice 2 tbsp. extra virgin olive oil, split 6 skinless chicken breast halves, sliced in half crosswise 1/2 cup Kalamata olives, pitted
- 1 1/2 pounds mustard greens, finely chopped (stalks removed) 1 cup white wine, dry
- medium red onion, halved and finely sliced 4 garlic cloves, crushed Sea salt
- peppercorns, ground
- For serving, lemon wedges

Directions:

- In a Dutch oven or big heavy pot, heat 1 tablespoon extra virgin olive oil over medium high heat.
- Season half of the chicken with salt and pepper and add to the saucepan; cook for approximately 8 minutes, or until browned on both sides.
- Place the cooked chicken on a platter and continue the process with the remaining chicken and oil.
- Reduce heat to medium and add the garlic and onion; cook, stirring occasionally, for approximately 6 minutes or until soft.
- Bring the chicken (along with any collected juices) and wine to a boil. Reduce heat to low and simmer for approximately 5 minutes, covered.
- Sprinkle the greens over the chicken and season with salt and pepper.
- Cook for another 5 minutes, covered, until the leaves have wilted and the chicken is opaque.

- Turn off the heat and add the olives and lemon juice.
- Serve with pan juices poured on top and lemon wedges on the side.

Chicken from the Mediterranean.

30 minutes to prepare.

Approximately 6 servings

Ingredients:

- 6 chicken breasts, skinned and deboned 3 garlic cloves, squeezed half cup onion, diced 3 cups tomatoes, chopped half cup Kalamata olives 1 tsp extra virgin olive oil half cup white wine, split
- 2 tsp. fresh thyme, minced Sea salt to taste 1/4 cup fresh parsley

Directions:

- In a pan, heat the oil and 3 tablespoons white wine over medium heat.
- Cook the chicken for 6 minutes on each side, or until browned.
- Remove the chicken from the pan and place it on a platter.
- In a pan, sauté the garlic and onions for 3 minutes before adding the tomatoes.
- Allow for five minutes of cooking time before lowering the heat and adding the remaining white wine and simmering for ten minutes.

- Cook for another 5 minutes after adding the thyme.
- Return the chicken to the skillet and cook over low heat until cooked through.
- Cook for a further minute after adding the olives and parsley. Season with salt and pepper before serving.

Salad with warm chicken and avocado.

Time to prepare: 20 minutes

Approximately 4 servings

Ingredients:

- 500g chicken breast fillets, 2 tbsp extra virgin olive oil, split
- 1 avocado, peeled and diced 2 chopped garlic cloves
- 1 teaspoon turmeric powder 3 tsp cumin powder
- 1 small broccoli head, chopped 1 big diced carrot
- currants, 1/3 cup
- 1/2 gallon chicken stock couscous, 1 1/2 cup a pinch of salt

Directions:

- 1 tablespoon extra virgin olive oil, heated in a large frying pan over medium heat; add chicken and cook for approximately 6 minutes each side or until cooked through; remove to a platter and keep warm.

- Meanwhile, in a heatproof dish, mix currants and couscous; whisk in boiling stock and put aside for at least 5 minutes, or until liquid is absorbed.

- Separate the grains with a fork.

- In a frying pan, add the remaining oil and the carrots; cook, stirring constantly, for approximately 1 minute.

- 1 minute after adding broccoli, toss in garlic, turmeric, and cumin. Remove the pan from the heat after another minute of cooking.

- Toss the broccoli combination with the chicken pieces, season with sea salt, and serve with the avocado on top.

Stew with chicken.

15 minutes to prepare.

Approximately 4 servings

Ingredients:

- 1 tablespoon olive oil (extra virgin)

- 3 boneless, skinless chicken breast halves (8 ounces each), chopped into tiny pieces

- Sea salt

- pepper, freshly ground 1 medium chopped onion 4 chopped garlic cloves 1/2 teaspoon dried oregano

- 1/2 pound escarole, trimmed and chopped 1 cup cooked whole-wheat couscous

- 1 can whole peeled tomatoes, pureed (28 ounces)

Directions:

- Heat extra virgin olive oil in a big heavy saucepan or Dutch oven over medium high heat.
- Season the chicken with salt and pepper.
- Cook chicken in batches in olive oil for approximately 5 minutes, flipping periodically, or until browned; transfer to a platter and set aside.
- Cook for approximately 10 minutes, or until the onion is gently browned, with the garlic and oregano, tomatoes, sea salt, and pepper.
- Cook, covered, for approximately 4 minutes or until the chicken is opaque.
- Fill the saucepan halfway with escarole and simmer until soft, approximately 4 minutes. Over couscous, serve the chicken stew.

Roasted Vegetables with Chicken

Time to prepare: 40 minutes.

Approximately 2 servings

Ingredients:

- 6 firm plum tomatoes, halved
- 1 red onion, cut into wedges yellow pepper, seeded and chopped into pieces
- 1 big zucchini, diagonally sliced
- 250g baby new potatoes, sliced
- 12 pitted black olives, skinless,

- boneless chicken breast fillets
- 1 tablespoon extra virgin olive oil
- 1 tablespoon green pesto

Directions:

- Preheat the oven to 4000 degrees Fahrenheit.
- In a roasting pan, layer zucchini, potatoes, tomatoes, onion, and pepper, then top with olives.
- Season with black pepper and sea salt.
- Each chicken breast should be cut into four pieces and placed on top of the veggies.
- Combine pesto and extra virgin olive oil in a small dish and distribute over the chicken. Cover with foil and bake for 30 minutes in a preheated oven.
- Return the pan to the oven and cook for another 10 minutes, or until the chicken is cooked through.
- Enjoy!

Olive Relish on Grilled Chicken

6 minute cook time

Approximately 4 servings

Ingredients:

- boneless, skinless chicken breast halves
- split 34 cup extra virgin olive oil Sea salt
- black pepper, freshly ground

- 1 small garlic clove, mashed with sea salt 2 tablespoons capers, washed and sliced half cup green olives, rinsed, pitted, and chopped quarter cup gently toasted almonds 1 tsp. fresh thyme, diced
- ½ teaspoon lemon zest
- 2 tbsp. fresh parsley, chopped

Directions:

- Preheat the grill to high.
- Drizzle 1 teaspoon extra virgin olive oil over 1 chicken breast on one side of a plastic wrap and fold the wrap over the chicken.
- Using a heavy sauté pan or a meat mallet, pound the chicken to approximately a half-inch thickness.
- Remove the plastic wrap and repeat the procedure with the remaining chicken.
- Season chicken with salt and pepper, then drizzle with 2 tablespoons extra virgin olive oil and let aside.
- Meanwhile, in a medium mixing bowl, add ½ cup extra virgin olive oil, capers, olives, almonds, garlic, thyme, lemon zest, and parsley.
- Transfer the chicken to a chopping board after grilling for approximately 3 minutes each side.
- Allow it cool slightly before cutting into half-inch thick pieces.
- Serve the relish beside the chicken pieces on four plates. Serve right away.

Turkey grilled with salsa

Time to prepare: 35 minutes.

Approximately 6 servings

Ingredients:

- For the spice rub, combine:
- a half teaspoon of garlic powder 1 teaspoon sweet paprika
- 1 teaspoon fennel seeds, crushed 2 teaspoons brown sugar
- 1 teaspoon salt
- freshly ground black pepper, half teaspoon
- To make the salsa:
- 1 tablespoon capers, drained
- 2 scant cups cherry tomatoes, diced half tbsp extra virgin olive oil quarter cup pimento-stuffed green olives, chopped 1 big garlic clove, minced 1 tablespoon fresh basil leaves 2 teaspoons lemon juice
- half teaspoon lemon zest, finely grated 6 cutlets of turkey breast
- 1 cup red onion, chopped Sea salt
- black pepper, freshly ground

Directions:

- In a small bowl, combine garlic powder, paprika, fennel seeds, brown sugar, salt, and pepper.
- Combine capers, olives, tomatoes, extra virgin olive oil, garlic, basil, lemon juice and zest, quarter teaspoon sea salt, and pepper in a separate bowl; leave aside.

- After immersing the meat in the spice rub, grill it for approximately 3 minutes each side over medium high heat, or until both sides are browned.

- Place the grilled turkey on a serving tray and let aside for 5 minutes to rest.

- Serve alongside salsa.

Olives, apricots, and cauliflower curried chicken

Time to prepare: 35 minutes.

Approximately 4 to 6 servings

Ingredients:

- 8 skinless, boneless chicken thighs quarter cup extra virgin olive oil, split half teaspoon ground cinnamon
- a quarter teaspoon of cayenne
- 1 tablespoon smoky paprika, divided 4 tablespoons curry powder 1 tablespoon apple cider vinegar to taste with sea salt
- 13 cup chopped fresh cilantro 1 head cauliflower, chopped 1 cup pitted green olives, halved 34 cup dried apricots, diced, soaked in boiling water and drained 6 slices of lemon

Directions:

- In a medium mixing bowl, combine the chicken thighs, 2 tablespoons extra virgin olive oil, cinnamon, cayenne, half teaspoon paprika, 2 tablespoons curry powder, vinegar, and sea salt; toss to coat and chill for approximately 8 hours, covered.

- Preheat the oven to 4500F and place the rack in the middle.

- Line a rimmed sheet pan with parchment paper; combine cauliflower, remaining olive oil, paprika, and curry powder in a large mixing bowl.

- Spread the mixture in a single layer with the olives and apricots.

- Place the marinated chicken on top of the cauliflower mixture, spacing them equally apart, and roast for 35 minutes, or until the chicken is cooked through and the cauliflower has browned.

- Serve the cauliflower and chicken with cilantro and lemon wedges on the side.

Salad of chicken with pine nuts, raisins, and fennel.

Time to cook: 0 minutes

1 big bowl (yield)

Ingredients:

To make the sauce:

- 1 tablespoon olive oil (extra virgin) 3 tablespoons of mayonnaise
- half a tiny garlic clove, mashed with salt 1 tsp cayenne
- 1 tablespoon lemon juice, freshly squeezed
- Salad ingredients:
- 3 tbsp. sweet onion, diced

- 13 cup fresh fennel, chopped 1 cup cooked shredded chicken golden raisins, 2 tbsp
- 2 tablespoons pine nuts, roasted
- 2 tablespoons fresh flat-leaf parsley, chopped Sea salt
- pepper, freshly ground

Directions:

- In a small bowl, whisk together extra virgin olive oil, mayonnaise, garlic, cayenne, and lemon juice.
- Mix onion, fennel, chicken, raisins, pine nuts, and parsley in a separate bowl; gently stir in the dressing and the Ingredients: together.
- Season with salt and pepper and chill for at least 1 hour before serving to let flavors to blend.

Rosemary Chicken in a Slow Cooker

7 hours and 10 minutes to cook

Approximately 8 servings

Ingredients:

- 1 small onion, finely sliced 4 garlic cloves, squeezed
- 2 tsp. dry rosemary 1 medium red bell pepper, sliced
- half teaspoon oregano, dried 2 sausages de porc

- 8 peeled, deboned, and split chicken breasts quarter teaspoon coarsely ground pepper quarter cup dry vermouth 1 tablespoon corn starch 2 tablespoons cold water

Directions:

- In a slow cooker, combine the onion, garlic, bell pepper, rosemary, and oregano.
- Remove the casings off the sausages and crumble them over the mixture.
- Sprinkle the chicken with pepper and arrange it in a single layer over the sausage.
- Slow-cook for 7 hours after adding the vermouth.
- Warm a large plate, then transfer the chicken to it and cover.
- In a small dish, combine the cornstarch and water, then stir into the liquid in the slow cooker.
- Cover and increase the heat. Cook for around ten minutes.

Penne with chicken.

30 minutes to prepare.

Approximately 4 servings

Ingredients:

- 1 pound of penne pasta 1 tablespoon butter
- 34 kg chicken breasts, deboned and skinned, sliced in half half cup red onion, diced 2 garlic cloves, crushed

2 tbsp. lemon juice 1 can artichoke hearts, soaked in water, diced half cup feta cheese, crumbled

- 1 diced tomato 3 tablespoons fresh parsley Sea salt
- black pepper, freshly ground 1 teaspoon dried oregano

Directions:

- In a large pot with salted boiling water, cook the penne pasta until al dente.
- In a large skillet over medium heat, melt the butter and add the onions and garlic.
- Cook for 2 minutes before adding the chicken.
- For approximately 6 minutes, stir regularly until the chicken is golden brown.
- Drain the artichoke hearts and combine with the cheese, lemon juice, tomatoes, oregano, parsley, and drained pasta in a pan. Reduce to medium low heat and cook for 3 minutes.
- Season with salt and pepper to taste, and serve immediately.

Kedgeree with Salmon and Vegetables

Time to prepare: 20 minutes

Ingredients:

- 7.5ml extra virgin olive oil 60ml basmati rice 2 teaspoons curry powder

- 100g flakes skinless hot-smoked salmon pieces 100 gram veggie mixture
- to taste with sea salt and pepper 1 finely sliced green onion

Directions:

- Add rice to a pot of boiling salted water, reduce heat to low, and simmer, covered, for 12 minutes or until just soft.
- In a medium saucepan, heat the extra virgin olive oil and sauté the onion, turning occasionally, until soft, approximately 3 minutes.
- Stir in the curry powder and simmer for 1 minute, or until aromatic.
- Stir in the rice until well incorporated, then add the salmon, veggies, salt, and pepper to taste.
- Cook for another 3 minutes, or until well heated. Serve.

Wilted Arugula with Grilled Sardines

Time to prepare: 10 minutes

4 servings

Ingredients:

- 16 fresh sardines, innards and gills removed 2 big bunches baby arugula, trimmed 2 tsp olive oil (extra virgin)
- Sea salt
- black pepper, freshly ground garnish with lemon wedges

Directions:

- Prepare an outside grill or a griddle on the stove.
- Rinse the arugula under running water, brush off the excess water, and place on a dish.
- Sardines should be rinsed and rubbed to remove scales, then dried and mixed with extra virgin olive oil in a big mixing basin.
- Toss to evenly coat.
- Grill the sardines for 3 minutes each side, or until golden brown and crispy.
- Season with salt and pepper and serve immediately on an arugula-lined dish.
- Serve immediately with lemon slices on the side.

Napa Slaw with Curry Salmon

45 minutes to prepare.

Approximately 4 servings

Ingredients:

- 1 cup basmati brown rice a pinch of salt, coarse
- a sprinkle of black pepper, ground
- 1 pound Napa cabbage (half head), cut crosswise 2 tbsp olive oil (extra virgin)
- quarter cup lime juice, freshly squeezed
- carrots, finely grated half cup fresh mint leaves 4 salmon filets (6 oz. each) 2 tablespoons curry powder
- Serve with lime wedges

Directions:

- In a large saucepan set over medium-low heat, bring two cups of water to a gentle boil; add rice and season with sea salt and pepper; reduce heat to low and simmer, covered, for approximately 35 minutes.
- Meanwhile, in a large mixing bowl, add Napa cabbage, extra virgin olive oil, lime juice, mint, carrots, salt, and black pepper; stir well.
- Preheat the broiler rack 4 inches from the heat source.
- Rub the salmon with curry, salt, and pepper on a baking sheet lined with foil.
- Broil for approximately 8 minutes, or until the salmon is just cooked through. Serve the prepared rice with grilled fish and a green salad.

Pasta with shrimp.

Time to cook: 5 minutes

Approximately 4 servings

Ingredients:

- a tablespoon of extra virgin olive oil 2 minced garlic cloves
- 2 cups chopped plum tomato quarter cup finely sliced fresh basil 1 pound peeled and deveined shrimp 2 tablespoons capers (drained)
- 13 cup Kalamata olives, pitted and chopped

- freshly ground black pepper, quarter teaspoon 4 cups angel hair pasta, cooked
- 1/4 cup feta cheese, crumbled Spray for cooking

Directions:

- Heat extra virgin olive oil in a large nonstick pan over medium high heat; add garlic and cook for approximately 30 seconds.
- Add the shrimp and cook for another minute.
- Reduce heat to medium low and add the tomato and basil; cook for approximately 3 minutes, or until the tomato is soft.
- Capers, Kalamata olives, and black pepper are added last.
- Toss the pasta and shrimp mixture in a large mixing bowl to incorporate, then sprinkle with cheese.
- Serve right away.

Fish Roasted

30 minutes to prepare.

Approximately 4 servings

Ingredients:

- 1 tablespoon extra virgin olive oil
- 1 (14-oz) can artichoke hearts, drained 4 garlic cloves, smashed
- 1 tiny green bell pepper sliced into strips

- half cup pitted olives, halved cherry tomatoes, 1 pint
- 1 teaspoon fennel
- 1 pound cod, quartered
- 4 tsp. orange peel, grated 2 tablespoons capers, drained
- 13 to 1/2 cup freshly squeezed orange juice a sprinkle of freshly ground pepper
- a dash of salt

Directions:

- Preheat the oven to 450 degrees Fahrenheit.
- 1 tablespoon olive oil, generously greased a 1015-inch baking pan
- In the preheated pan, arrange the artichoke hearts, garlic, bell pepper, olives, tomatoes, and fennel seed.
- Serve the fish with orange peel, capers, orange juice, pepper, and salt on top of the veggies.

Fish Baked

Time to prepare: 50 minutes.

Approximately 4 servings

Ingredients:

- 2 tsp olive oil (extra virgin) 1 big onion, sliced
- 1/4 cup orange juice 1 tablespoon orange zest
- lemon juice, quarter cup

- a quarter-cup of apple juice
- 1 garlic clove, minced
- 1 (16-ounce) can whole tomatoes, drained and finely chopped, with the liquid set aside
- half-cup tomato juice set aside crushed dried basil half teaspoon crushed dry thyme half teaspoon crushed dried oregano 1 teaspoon fennel seeds, crushed black pepper, a pinch
- 1 pound of fish fillets (perch, flounder or sole)

Directions:

- In a large nonstick skillet, heat the oil over medium heat. Cook for 5 minutes or until the onion is soft in the oil. Stir in the remaining ingredients. Except for the fish, the ingredients are as follows.
- Cook for approximately 30 minutes, uncovered.
- Place the fish in a baking dish and pour the sauce over it.
- Bake the fish for 15 minutes at 375°F, uncovered, or until it flakes readily when checked with a fork.

Cod from Spain.

15 minutes to prepare.

Approximately 6 servings

Ingredients:

- 1 tablespoon olive oil (extra virgin) 1 tablespoon butter

- quarter cup finely chopped onion 1 cup tomato sauce 2 tablespoons garlic, diced
- ½ cup deli marinated Italian vegetable salad, drained and sliced 15 cherry tomatoes, halved 1 teaspoon cayenne
- 1 pinch of black pepper 1 paprika dash
- 6 fillets of cod

Directions:

- Place the olive oil and butter in a large pan over medium heat.
- Cook the onion and garlic until the garlic begins to brown. Allow the tomatoes and tomato sauce to boil.
- Combine the marinated veggies, olives, and spices in a mixing bowl.
- Cook the fillet for 8 minutes in the sauce over medium heat. Serve right away.

Burgers with Greek Salmon.

15 minutes to prepare.

Approximately 4 servings

Ingredients:

- 1 pound sliced skinless salmon fillets 1/2 cup panko 1 big egg white
- 1 tsp. freshly ground black pepper 1 sprinkle sea salt
- cucumber slices, half a cup

- 1/4 cup feta cheese, crumbled
- 4 toasted ciabatta breads (2.5 oz)

Directions:

- Combine the salmon, egg white, and panko in a food processor and pulse until the salmon is finely minced.
- Season the salmon mixture with salt and pepper and form four 4-inch patties.
- Preheat the grill to medium-high and cook the patties for approximately 7 minutes each side, rotating once, or until just cooked through.
- Serve with buns and your favorite toppings (such sliced cucumbers and feta).

Tuna grilled

6 minute cook time

Approximately 4 servings

Ingredients:

- 4 1/2-inch thick tuna steaks half cup soaked hickory wood chips 3 tablespoons extra virgin olive oil Sea salt
- black pepper, freshly ground 1 lime's juice

Directions:

- Refrigerate for an hour after placing the tuna and olive oil in a zip lock plastic bag.
- Make a charcoal or gas grill ready.

- To add flavor to a coal barbecue, toss a handful of hickory wood chips over the hot coals.
- Grease the grill grate lightly.
- Season the tuna with salt and pepper and cook for 6 minutes on the grill, flipping once.
- Place on a platter to cool.
- Serve the fish right away with a lime juice drizzle.

Simple Fish Dish

30 minutes to prepare.

Approximately 4 servings

Ingredients:

- 4 halibut fillets (6 ounces) a tablespoon of Greek seasoning
- 1 teaspoon of lemon juice
- quarter cup capers quarter cup olive oil
- 1 jar (5 oz.) Kalamata olives, pitted 1 onion, chopped
- 1 big sliced tomato
- a sprinkle of black pepper, freshly ground salt to taste

Directions:

- Preheat the oven to 250 degrees Fahrenheit.
- Sprinkle the Greek spice over the halibut fillets on an aluminum foil sheet.

- Combine lemon juice, olive oil, capers, olives, onion, tomato, salt, and pepper in a mixing bowl; spread the mixture over the fillets and fold the foil edges to close.
- Bake for 40 minutes, or until the fish flakes easily when forked.

Stir-fried salmon with beans

Time to prepare: 10 minutes

Approximately 4 servings

Ingredients:

- 1 teaspoon crushed red pepper 5ml rice wine 2.5g cornstarch
- 7.5 mL garlic-black bean sauce 7.5 milliliters rice vinegar
- 30ml water cup Canola oil, 5 mL
- 100g peeled, diced salmon 10g sliced scallions
- Bean sprouts, 90g

Directions:

- Crushed red pepper, cornstarch, rice wine, bean-garlic sauce, vinegar, and water in a mixing bowl until thoroughly blended.
- In a medium-sized skillet, heat the oil. Cook for 2 minutes after adding the fish.
- Combine the sauce, scallions, and sprouts in a mixing bowl.

- Cook for 3 minutes, or until the sprouts are tender and the liquid has evaporated.

Flounder, Mediterranean

30 minutes to prepare.

Approximately 4 servings

Ingredients:

- 5 tomatoes, Roma
- 2 tbsp olive oil (extra virgin)
- 1/2 a chopped onion
- 2 chopped garlic cloves 1 tablespoon Italian seasoning
- flounder/tilapia/halibut, 1 pound
- 4 tablespoons capers
- 24 pitted and chopped Kalamata olives 1 teaspoon lemon juice, freshly squeezed
- white wine, quarter cup
- 6 fresh basil leaves, minced; 3 tablespoons Parmigiano-Reggiano

Directions:

- Preheat the oven to 4250 degrees Fahrenheit.
- Place the tomatoes in a dish of cold water after plunging them into boiling water; remove the skins and cut the tomatoes.
- In a pan over medium heat, add extra virgin olive oil and sauté onions until transparent.

- Cook until tomatoes are soft, stirring in garlic and Italian seasoning.
- Combine the wine, lemon juice, capers, olives, and half of the basil in a mixing bowl.
- Reduce the heat to low and whisk in the Parmesan cheese; simmer for 15 minutes, or until the sauce is bubbling and heated.
- Place the fish in a baking dish with the sauce and bake for approximately 20 minutes, or until the fish is cooked through.

Olives, tomatoes, and capers with fish

Time to cook: 16 minutes

Approximately 4 servings

Ingredients:

- 4 (5-ounce) sea bass fillets 4 tsp extra virgin olive oil, split
- 1/2 cup white wine 1 small onion, chopped 2 tablespoons capers
- 1 cup chopped tomatoes with juice from a can
- quarter teaspoon crushed red pepper cups half cup pitted black olives baby spinach leaves, fresh seasonings (salt and pepper)

Directions:

- In a large nonstick pan over medium high heat, heat 2 teaspoons extra virgin olive oil.

- Cook for 3 minutes each side, or until fish is opaque in the middle.
- Warm the cooked fish by placing it on a platter.
- In the same pan, add the remaining oil and sauté the onion for approximately 2 minutes, or until transparent.
- Cook for approximately 2 minutes, or until the liquid has been reduced by half.
- Cook for another 3 minutes after adding the capers, tomatoes, olives, and red pepper.
- Cook, stirring constantly for 3 minutes or until the spinach has silted. Stir in the salt and pepper, then pour the sauce over the fish.
- Serve right away.

Cod (Mediterranean)

Time to prepare: 35 minutes.

Approximately 4 servings

Ingredients:

- 1 tablespoon olive oil (extra virgin) 100g minced onion, frozen 1 tablespoon chopped frozen garlic
- 230g chopped Italian tomatoes from a can 1 tablespoon pureed tomatoes
- Cod fillets, skinless and boneless, 400g pack tbsp. chopped frozen parsley 200g frozen mixed peppers 50g black olives, pitted
- 800g frozen white rice packet

Directions:

- In a medium saucepan, heat extra virgin olive oil; add onion and sauté for approximately 3 minutes.
- Sauté for another 2 minutes, or until garlic is aromatic.
- Bring to a slow boil with the tomatoes, tomato puree, and water.
- Reduce heat to low and cook for approximately 20 minutes, or until the sauce has thickened.
- Return to a boil with the cod and peppers; poke the fish into the sauce a little and return to a simmer for approximately 8 minutes.
- Cook for another 2 minutes after adding the parsley and olives. Meanwhile, cook the rice according to the package directions.
- Serve the fish over steaming rice.

Salmon grilled

Time to cook: 8 minutes

Approximately 4 servings

Ingredients:

- lemon juice, freshly squeezed 1 teaspoon garlic, minced
- 1 tablespoon fresh parsley, chopped 4 tbsp. fresh basil, chopped
- 4 ounces each salmon fillet Is extra virgin olive oil available?

- to taste with sea salt and crushed black pepper 4 chopped green olives
- black pepper, cracked 4 thin lemon slices

Directions:

- Fire grill to medium high and lightly cover grill rack with olive oil cooking spray and place 4 inches from heat.
- In a small bowl, combine the lemon juice, minced garlic, parsley, and basil.
- Season the fish with sea salt and pepper after coating it in extra virgin olive oil.
- Place each fish fillet on the hot grill, herb-side down, with an equal quantity of garlic mixture on top.
- Grill for approximately 4 minutes over high heat, or until the edges become white; flip and transfer the fish to aluminum foil.
- Reduce the heat to low and cook for another 4 minutes.
- Serve the grilled fish with lemon slices and green olives as a garnish.
- Serve right away.

Apple and onion with liver

Time to prepare: 25 minutes.

Approximately 2 servings

Ingredients:

- Spray with extra virgin olive oil

- onion, half pound
- 2 apples, Granny Smith 1 cup of liquid
- 1 tablespoon lemon juice 1 tablespoon wine vinegar 1 teaspoon of brown sugar
- fresh rosemary, plus sprigs for decoration 2 tablespoons currants 2 tablespoons unsalted butter 8 ounces of calf liver
- white wine, quarter cup
- a quarter teaspoon of salt spritz with olive oil

Directions:

- Preheat the oven to 2000 degrees Fahrenheit.
- Set a pan over medium heat and coat with extra virgin olive oil spray; add onions and sauté for approximately 4 minutes, or until transparent.
- Cook for approximately 5 minutes, or until the apples begin to color. Cook until apples are soft, stirring in water, lemon juice, vinegar, and sugar.
- Cook, stirring constantly for approximately 2 minutes, then divide over two dishes and keep warm in the oven.
- In the same pan, melt the butter until it foams.
- Stir in the liver and cook for approximately 10 minutes, or until the exterior is browned.
- Distribute the liver amongst the two apple-onion plates.
- Deglaze the pan with white wine; simmer until the liquid is reduced by half, then pour an equal quantity over

each dish.

- Serve with fresh rosemary on top.

Chops of lamb

Time to prepare: 10 minutes

Approximately 4 servings

Ingredients:

- 1 tablespoon oregano, dry 1 tablespoon chopped garlic, quarter teaspoon black pepper, freshly ground half teaspoon sea salt
- 8 lamb loin chops, fat removed tbsp. lemon juice, fresh Spray for cooking

Directions:

- Preheat the oven's broiler.
- Combine all of the spices, herbs, and lemon juice in a small dish and massage it all over the lamb chops.
- Broil the lamb chops for 4 minutes on each side or until done to your liking on a broiler pan sprayed with cooking spray.
- Cover the cooked lamb chops with foil and set aside for 5 minutes before serving.

Calf's Liver with Sage.

Time to prepare: 10 minutes

Approximately 4 servings

Ingredients:

- 2 tsp olive oil (extra virgin) 8 ounces calves' liver, sliced into tiny strips 1 garlic clove, minced 1 tablespoon parsley (flat leaf)
- 1 tablespoon sage, fresh
- 1 tablespoon balsamic vinegar 2 tablespoons red wine 2 tablespoons unsalted butter
- 1 teaspoon lemon juice
- a quarter teaspoon of salt peppercorns

Directions:

- In a nonstick pan over medium heat, heat extra virgin olive oil; add minced garlic and cook for 3 minutes, or until transparent and aromatic.
- Cook for 5 minutes, or until the liver strips, parsley, and sage are charred on the exterior.
- Transfer the liver to a heated platter and deglaze the pan for approximately 30 seconds with vinegar, red wine, butter, and lemon juice.
- Serve immediately after pouring the sauce over the meat.

Burgers with seasoned lamb.

Time to prepare: 10 minutes

Approximately 4 servings

Ingredients:

- 1 pound of ground lamb 1 teaspoon cumin, 1/2 teaspoon cinnamon 1 teaspoon ginger powder

- split ¼ cup extra virgin olive oil
- 1 teaspoon freshly ground black pepper; ¼ cup fresh cilantro, split 2 tbsp. oregano, fresh
- quarter cup fresh flat leaf parsley tiny garlic clove, squeezed 34 teaspoon red pepper flakes, crushed sherry vinegar (1 tablespoon)
- reheated and halved pitas tomato slices
- 1 8 oz plain Greek yogurt package

Directions:

- Build a fire on a charcoal or gas barbecue.
- Cumin, cinnamon, ginger, 1 tablespoon extra virgin olive oil, and half teaspoon black pepper are combined with ground lamb.
- Mix well and divide into four burgers.
- Grill the burgers for 5 minutes on each side after spraying the grill with olive oil.
- In a food processor, combine the remaining olive oil, cilantro, oregano, garlic, red pepper flakes, parsley, and vinegar until a thick paste forms.
- Serve each burger with sliced tomato, the processed sauce, and a dollop of yogurt on a dish.

London Broil with Mushrooms Sautéed in Bourbon

Time to prepare: 60 minutes

Approximately 3 servings

Ingredients:

- extra virgin olive oil, half a teaspoon
- half a cup shallots, minced
- 34 poundcrimini mushrooms, halved 6 tbsp beef stock (non-fat)
- 3 tablespoons bourbon
- half a tablespoon of unsalted butter
- 1 tablespoon maple syrup to taste black pepper
- 1 pound. lean Broil in London
- 18 teaspoon salt

Directions:

- Preheat the oven to 400 degrees Fahrenheit.
- For approximately 10 minutes, heat a nonstick pan in the oven. Remove the pan from the heat and whisk in extra virgin olive oil to coat it.
- Return the pan to the oven and roast the mushrooms for approximately 15 minutes, stirring once with a wooden spatula.
- Return the skillet to the oven and stir in the beef stock, bourbon, butter, maple syrup, and pepper; mix and simmer for another 10 minutes, or until the liquid has reduced by half.
- Place the pan in the oven and put it aside.
- Heat another nonstick skillet for approximately 10 minutes in the oven.
- Meanwhile, season the steak with salt and pepper before placing it in the heated pan.

- Roast for about 14 minutes, flipping once. Warm the mushrooms while the meat is removed from the oven.

- Place the steak on a chopping board and let aside for 5 minutes to rest. To serve, thinly slice the meat and top with sautéed mushrooms.

Kabobs of grilled lamb with sage.

30 minutes to prepare.

Approximately 2 servings

Ingredients:

- 1 tablespoon lemon juice 2 tablespoons chives
- fresh flat leaf parsley, 1 tablespoon 2 tbsp. sage leaves
- 1 tablespoon brown sugar
- 1 tablespoon olive oil (extra virgin) 2 tablespoons sherry
- 1 tablespoon maple syrup
- a quarter teaspoon of salt
- 8 oz. lean shoulder lamb 2 quarts of water
- 4 red potatoes, medium cut into half a white onion 6 caps of shitake mushrooms
- red bell pepper, half

Directions:

- Lemon juice, chives, parsley, sage, brown sugar, extra virgin olive oil, sherry, maple syrup, and salt in a blender; purée until smooth.

- Cut the lamb into 8 cubes and place it in a zip bag with the marinade. Refrigerate for at least 4 hours.
- Bring a large saucepan of water to a boil.
- Steam for 15 minutes after cutting potatoes in half and adding half an onion to the saucepan. Remove from the heat and set aside to cool.
- Chop the remaining onion and pepper into small pieces.
- Alternate the lamb cube, mushroom cap, pepper, onion, and potato on a skewer.
- Set aside the marinade.
- Turn the kabobs every 3 minutes over a hot grill, basting with the remaining marinade.

Lentils with Lemony Pork

30 minutes to prepare.

Approximately 4 servings

Ingredients:

- 4 (4 ounce) pork chops 2 tbsp extra virgin olive oil, split
- 2 tablespoons lemon juice 1 teaspoon lemon zest fresh rosemary tbsp. garlic 1 tablespoon of parsley
- 1 tablespoon maple syrup ½ cup green lentils in 6 cups water 1 shallot
- 1 celery rib
- split ½ cup dry sherry 1 tablespoon unsalted butter 1 teaspoon sea salt

- 1/4 teaspoon red pepper flakes

Directions:

- Refrigerate for at least 8 hours after combining extra virgin olive oil, pork chops, lemon juice, lemon zest, garlic clove, rosemary, parsley, and maple syrup in a zipper bag.
- In a medium saucepan, combine 3 cups water and green lentils; simmer for approximately 20 minutes, or until lentils are just cooked; drain and rinse.
- Preheat the oven to 3500 degrees Fahrenheit.
- Heat the marinade in a nonstick pan over medium high heat; sear the pork for approximately 2 minutes each side, then move the skillet to the oven.
- Meanwhile, in a second nonstick pan over medium high heat, heat 1 teaspoon extra virgin olive oil; add shallot, red pepper flakes, and celery and reduce heat to medium; cook for approximately 4 minutes or until tender. Warm the lentils by stirring them in.
- Cook for approximately 2 minutes, or until liquid is reduced by half, with a quarter teaspoon of sea salt and a quarter cup of sherry. Melt the butter in a separate bowl.
- Divide the lentil mixture among four dishes and top with one pork chop from the first pan for each serving.
- Remove and discard the garlic cloves from the marinade in the first skillet, then deglaze with 1/4 cup sherry and 1/4 teaspoon sea salt; simmer until the liquid has reduced by half.
- Pour the sauce over each plate in an even layer and serve.

Pork Chops with Cumin.

Time to prepare: 20 minutes

Serving Size: 1

Ingredients:

- 4-ounce pork chop, center-cut
- 18 teaspoon salt
- 18 teaspoon cumin powder Oil from olives 1 tablespoon mashed avocado
- 2 tablespoons cilantro leaves

Directions:

- Preheat the oven to 400 degrees Fahrenheit.
- Over medium heat, heat a large skillet.
- Meanwhile, season the pork chop with salt and cumin.
- Add the seasoned pork chop to the pan after spraying it with extra virgin olive oil.
- Cook for approximately 10 minutes in the oven, then flip the pork chop and sprinkle the charred side with avocado.
- Return to the oven and cook for another 10 minutes, or until the pork is cooked through.
- Over mashed potatoes, serve the pork topped with cilantro.

Lamb Burgers

Time to prepare: 10 minutes

Approximately 4 servings

Ingredients:

- extra virgin olive oil, 1 tablespoon 1 pound lean ground lamb 1 tablespoon yogurt
- 18 teaspoon allspice powder
- half a cup chopped cilantro leaves 1 shallot, finely chopped 2 garlic cloves, chopped 1 teaspoon fresh ginger, minced 18 tsp ground cumin 1 red chili pepper, chopped 4 seeds of cardamom
- ¼ teaspoon sea salt 18 teaspoon black pepper olive oil spray
- 4 hamburger buns (whole wheat)

Directions:

- Refrigerate for at least 20 minutes after combining all ingredients (excluding spray olive oil and buns).
- Preheat the oven to 400 degrees Fahrenheit.
- In a large nonstick skillet, heat extra virgin olive oil over medium heat.
- Meanwhile, shape the lamb mixture into four patties.
- Sear burgers for approximately 1 minute in prepared pan; place to preheated oven and cook for about 5 minutes; flip burgers and cook for another 3 minutes.

Steak with herb-maple crust.

Time to prepare: 10 minutes

Approximately 4 servings

Ingredients:

- 3 tablespoons rosemary
- 3 tbsp. tarragon (fresh) 3 tablespoons chives
- 3 tablespoons oregano, chopped 4 tablespoons parsley
- 3 tablespoons of maple syrup (4 ounce) trimmed ribeye steaks
- spritz olive oil half teaspoon sea salt quarter teaspoon black pepper

Directions:

- Preheat the oven to 450 degrees Fahrenheit.
- In the oven, heat a nonstick skillet.
- Meanwhile, on a dish, mix the minced herbs. In a separate dish, pour the maple syrup.
- Season the steak with salt and pepper before dipping it into the maple syrup and turning it to evenly cover it.
- Turn the steak to cover it completely with the herbs. Rep with the rest of the meat.
- Remove the skillet from the oven and spray it with extra virgin olive oil; add the steaks and flip them until fully seared.
- Return to oven and cook for another 4 minutes, then flip and cook for another 6 minutes.

Blue Cheese Butter on Tenderloin

15 minutes to prepare.

Approximately 2 servings

Ingredients:

- 1/8 teaspoon black pepper
- minced tiny shallot 1 tablespoon salted butter
- 1 tablespoon parsley, chopped 2 tablespoons blue cheese
- Spray with extra virgin olive oil
- 2 4-ounce filets of beef tenderloin quarter teaspoon of salt

Directions:

- Blend pepper, shallot, butter, parsley, and blue cheese until creamy in a blender.
- Preheat the oven to 450 degrees Fahrenheit.
- Spray a nonstick pan with extra virgin olive oil and place it in the oven. Season the beef with salt and pepper and set it in the pan; cook for approximately 7 minutes, then flip and cook for another 4 minutes.
- To serve, place the meat on a platter and top with seasoned butter.

Beef with Green Curry.

Time to prepare: 40 minutes.

Approximately 3 servings

Ingredients:

- 1 tablespoon olive oil (extra virgin)
- 1 cup cilantro leaves half cup chopped parsley
- 1 chopped white onion 1 chopped fresh Thai green chili 2 garlic cloves, finely sliced 1/4 teaspoon turmeric 1/2 teaspoon cumin 2 tablespoons lime juice 1/4 teaspoon salt peppercorns
- 16 oz. top round beef, chopped into tiny pieces 1 can coconut milk (light)
- 1 teaspoon turmeric
- 1/2 teaspoon cumin powder 1/4 teaspoon salt

Directions:

- Curry paste (green):
- Combine extra virgin olive oil, parsley, cilantro, onion, chili pepper, garlic, turmeric, cumin, lime juice, sea salt, and pepper in a food processor or blender; process until very smooth.
- Toss the steak with the green curry paste in a bowl to coat. Refrigerate for 30 minutes at least.
- When ready, brown the beef in a large pan over medium-high heat with the green curry sauce.
- Reduce heat to low and stir for approximately 10 minutes, or until the exterior of the beef is browned.
- Cook, stirring occasionally, for approximately 30 minutes, or until the sauce has thickened.
- Serve right away.

Pork Roasted with Balsamic Reduction.

Time to prepare: 40 minutes Approximately 6 servings

Ingredients:

- 1 teaspoon olive oil (extra virgin) ¼ cup chopped yellow onion 1 garlic clove, minced
- 12 cup low-sodium vegetable or chicken broth 1/4 cup balsamic vinegar 1/4 cup port 1/4 cup dried cherries
- half cup quarter cup low-fat sour cream 2 percent milk
- 34 pound trimmed pork tenderloin

Directions:

- In a medium saucepan placed over medium high heat, heat extra virgin olive oil; add garlic and onion and sauté for 3 minutes or until tender.
- Cook until the sauce is reduced to half cup by adding the chicken stock, balsamic vinegar, port, and dried cherries.
- Scrape the sauce into a blender and puree until smooth; add the milk and sour cream and return to the pan, stirring constantly until heated through.
- Preheat the oven to 375 degrees Fahrenheit.
- Place pork tenderloin on a roasting pan and cook for 15 minutes in the oven.
- Remove the pork from the oven and let it rest for 5 minutes before slicing it into tiny pieces. Over 3 tablespoons of sauce, serve the meat.

Pitas with Mediterranean Beef

Time to cook: 5 minutes

Approximately 4 servings

Ingredients:

- 1 pound beef mince
- black pepper, freshly ground 3/4 cup store-bought hummus sea salt half teaspoon dried oregano tbsp extra virgin olive oil, split quarter tiny red onion, sliced 2 tbsp. flat-leaf parsley, fresh 4 pitas
- 4 slices of lemon

Directions:

- Season beef with a quarter teaspoon of ground pepper, half teaspoon of sea salt, and oregano.
- In a pan set over medium heat, add 1 tablespoon extra virgin olive oil and cook the beef patties for approximately 2 minutes each side, or until lightly browned.
- To serve, layer the beef patties, hummus, parsley, and onion on top of pitas, then drizzle with the remaining extra virgin olive oil and lemon wedges.

Meat Loaf with Parmesan.

Time to prepare: 50 minutes.

Approximately 4 servings

Ingredients:

- ground beef, half pound
- bread crumbs (half cup)

- half a cup flat-leaf parsley, chopped 1 onion, grated
- quarter cup tomato paste big egg half cup grated Parmesan Sea salt
- black pepper, freshly ground

Directions:

- Preheat the oven to 4000 degrees Fahrenheit. Combine ground beef, bread crumbs, parsley, onion, egg, Parmesan cheese, tomato paste, sea salt, and pepper in a large mixing bowl.
- Cover a baking sheet with foil and flatten the meat mixture into an 8-inch loaf.
- Bake for 50 minutes or until well done in a preheated oven.

Steak with Mediterranean Flank.

Time to prepare: 40 minutes.

Approximately 4 to 6 servings

- 1 tablespoon fragrant herbs, chopped (marjoram, rosemary, sage, thyme, or a mix)
- 2 garlic cloves, minced
- 2 tbsp olive oil (extra virgin) 1 teaspoon of salt
- 1 teaspoon black pepper, ground
- 12 cup Greek vinaigrette 12 pound flank steak, trimmed

Directions:

- Combine herbs, garlic, extra virgin olive oil, sea salt, and pepper in a small bowl; rub over the steak and let aside for 20 minutes.

- Meanwhile, preheat your gas grill over medium-high heat.

- For even cooking, grill the steak for approximately 15 minutes, rotating it every 4 minutes.

- Transfer the grilled steak to a cutting board and let aside for 5 minutes to rest before slicing into tiny pieces and plating.

- Serve immediately with vinaigrette drizzled over top.

Chops of Mediterranean Lamb

1 hour to prepare.

Approximately 4 servings

Ingredients:

- divided tbsp extra virgin olive oil 3 cloves garlic
- 1 teaspoon fresh rosemary, chopped 2 tbsp. fresh mint, chopped
- 4 lamb chops, lean
- 3 oz. crumbled feta cheese 2 yellow peppers, diced 2 red peppers, diced 4 zucchinis, sliced 1 eggplant, sliced Cherry tomatoes, 9 oz.

Directions:

- Preheat the oven to 3500 degrees Fahrenheit.

- 1 tablespoon extra virgin olive oil, garlic, rosemary, and mint, blended until smooth in a food processor; spread over lamb chops.

- Combine peppers, zucchini, and eggplant on a baking sheet and sprinkle with the remaining oil.

- Place the lamb chops on top of the veggies and bake for approximately 25 minutes in a preheated oven.

- Remove the baking sheet from the oven and cover with cherry tomatoes and feta cheese; return to oven and roast for another 10 minutes, or until the lamb chops are cooked through and the cheese has started to brown.

- With lamb chops and a green salad, serve the roasted veggies.

Beef and Broccoli are both nutritious.

Time to prepare: 20 minutes

Ingredients:

- 8ml vegetable oil, split 100g finely cut flank steak 90g broccoli florets 7.5g corn starch 60ml water

- 1 finely sliced green onion 1/2 shallots, cut finely 1 small garlic clove, minced 1 teaspoon red pepper flakes, crushed 1 g fresh ginger, minced

- 5ml honey

- 20 milliliters soy sauce

Directions:

- In a medium-sized skillet, heat the oil.

- Cook for approximately 8 minutes, or until the meat is browned. Set the steak aside after removing it from the pan.
- In the same pan, sauté the green onions, shallots, and garlic for 1 minute, stirring constantly.
- Cook for 5 minutes after adding the broccoli.
- In a mixing basin, whisk together cornstarch and water until smooth.
- Combine the red pepper flakes, ginger, honey, and soy sauce in a separate dish; whisk in the cornstarch mixture until thoroughly blended.
- Cook for approximately 5 minutes, or until the sauce has thickened. Cook for 3 minutes after adding the meat.
- Over brown rice, serve.

Chapter Seven
Vegetarian Recipes and Appetizers

Beans with Stewed Artichokes

25 minutes to cook

Serves four

Ingredients:

- 1 pound shelled fava beans
- 3 tablespoons lemon juice, freshly squeezed 4 c.
- Artichokes (baby): 24
- 1 ½ lemon, rubbed on artichokes 2 tsp olive oil, extra virgin
- 4 flat-leave parsley sprigs fresh thyme, 4 sprigs
- crushed red pepper flakes (about 1/4 teaspoon) 1 tsp. black pepper, freshly ground 1 tablespoon of salt
- 3 garlic cloves, peeled and smashed garlic 1 ½ lemon, rubbed on artichokes

Directions:

- Set aside a big basin filled with ice and water.
- In a medium saucepan, fill halfway with water and bring to a boil over high heat. 30 seconds after adding the fava beans, blanch them.
- Remove the beans from the boiling water and place them in an ice bath for 5 minutes or until they are completely chilled.

- Set aside the fava beans with their skins peeled.

- Set lemon juice and 4 cups water aside in a large mixing basin. Cut the tops off the artichokes and remove the tough outer leaves.

- Trim the stems and peels from each stem and drop them in the lemon-water combination after rubbing them with the half of a lemon.

- In a saucepan over medium heat, heat extra virgin olive oil until it is heated but not smoky.

- Cook, stirring constantly, for 2 minutes, or until the shallot is lightly caramelized.

- Bring the mixture to a slow simmer with the artichokes, parsley, and thyme, as well as 1 cup of the lemon-water combination.

- Reduce to a low heat and continue to cook, covered, for another 14 minutes or until the artichokes are soft.

- Cook for 3 more minutes, or until the fava beans are soft. Instantly serve.

Pasta with artichokes, tomatoes, and olives from the Mediterranean.

20 minutes to cook

Serves four

Ingredients:

- 12 oz spaghetti (whole wheat)
- 2 tablespoons extra virgin olive oil (distributed) 1 medium onion, finely cut lengthwise 2 garlic cloves, sliced salt and pepper, coarsely ground

- white wine, half a cup
- 1 washed and chopped lengthwise artichoke heart
- 13 cup pitted Kalamata olives, split lengthwise half cup fresh basil leaves, torn quarter cup grated Parmesan cheese, plus extra for serving

Directions:

- Cook pasta until al dente according to package directions in a large saucepan of boiling salted water; drain and set aside 1 cup pasta water.
- Fill the saucepan with the cooked pasta.
- Meanwhile, heat 1 tablespoon extra virgin olive oil; add garlic and onion, season with sea salt and black pepper, and sauté for approximately 4 minutes, stirring often.
- Cook for another 2 minutes, or until all of the liquid has evaporated.
- Cook for another 3 minutes, or until the artichoke begins to brown.
- Cook for 2 minutes after adding half the tomatoes and olives.
- Add the pasta and toss with the remaining olive oil, tomatoes, basil, and cheese, if preferred.
- Serve with additional cheese on the side.

Olives, Swiss Chard

15 minutes to prepare

Serves four

Ingredients:

- Swiss chard, ¼ pound, washed and trimmed 1 teaspoon olive oil, extra virgin
- 13 cup Kalamata olives (brine-cured), pitted and coarsely chopped half cup water 1 garlic clove, sliced 1 small yellow onion, diced 1 jalapeño pepper, chopped

Directions:

- Cut the stems into tiny pieces and coarsely slice the leaves of Swiss chard; keep aside.
- In a Dutch oven or big pan over medium heat, heat extra virgin olive oil.
- Sauté for 6 minutes, or until onion is soft and transparent.
- Cook for approximately 3 minutes, covered, with olives, Swiss chard stems, and water.
- Cook for another 4 minutes, covered, until the chard leaves and stems are soft.
- Instantly serve.

Tagine with Grilled Veggies

50 minutes to cook

6 portion size

Ingredients:

- golden raisins (quarter cup)
- 2/3 cup uncooked couscous 6 tiny red potatoes, quartered 1 tsp. extra virgin olive oil 2 garlic cloves, squeezed 1

big red onion, wedged 1 tsp. fennel seeds, crushed 1/4 tsp. cinnamon, ground 1 tsp. cumin, crushed 1 1/2 cups water 1/4 cup pitted and sliced green olives spray for cooking

- 1 green bell pepper, chopped
- half-can tomatoes, diced 2 tsp balsamic vinegar

Directions:

- Make a charcoal or gas grill ready.
- In a zip lock plastic bag, mix the bell peppers, red onion, quarter teaspoon sea salt, vinegar, and half teaspoon olive oil.
- Add the remaining olive oil, garlic, and chopped onion to a large nonstick saucepan over medium heat.
- Add fennel, cumin, and cinnamon and cook for another 3 minutes. Allow for another minute of cooking before adding the remaining salt, olives, raisins, potatoes, tomatoes, black pepper, and water to the pan and bringing to a boil.
- Cook for 25 minutes, or until the potatoes are cooked, covered.
- Remove the onions and bell peppers from the plastic bag and cook for approximately 10 minutes on a grill rack sprayed with cooking spray.
- In a separate saucepan, bring the remaining water to a boil and add the couscous gently.
- Remove the pan from the heat and cover it for 5 minutes to cool. Top with grilled onions, bell peppers, and pine nuts and serve over couscous.

Pilau de Chorizos

40 minutes to cook

Serves four

Ingredients:

- 1 tablespoon olive oil, extra virgin
- 4 garlic cloves, minced 1 teaspoon smoked paprika
- 1/4 kilo basmati rice 1 can tomatoes, diced
- half liter stock 4 garlic cloves, minced
- 1 parsley bunch, cut 1 lemon zest, peeled in thick strips and wedged fresh bay leaves

Directions:

- Pour the oil into a large saucepan set over medium heat.
- Cook for approximately 6 minutes, or until the onion becomes golden brown. Push the onions to one side of the pan, add the chorizo, and heat until some of the oils begin to release.
- Following that will be the garlic and paprika.
- After 2 minutes of stirring, add the tomatoes and simmer for another 5 minutes. Pour in the stock, rice, lemon zest, and bay leaves.
- Bring to a boil while stirring everything in the pan. Simmer for 12 minutes with the lid off.
- Turn off the heat, remove the lid, and cover the pan with foil for 15 minutes.
- Serve with lemon wedges after incorporating the parsley. (The lemon juice adds a wonderful flavor to the meal.)

Garbanzos, Raisins, and Spinach Pasta

25 minutes to cook

6 portion size

Ingredients:

- Farfalle (bow tie) pasta, 8 ounces 2 tbsp olive oil, extra virgin
- half a cup chicken broth 4 smashed garlic cloves (unsalted)
- Garbanzo beans, washed and drained, half a can (19 ounces) fresh spinach, chopped
- golden raisins (half cup)
- 2 tablespoons parmesan peppercorns, cracked

Directions:

- Bring a saucepan of salted water to a roaring boil over high heat.
- Cook for 12 minutes, or until the pasta is al dente; drain and leave aside.
- In a large pan, heat extra virgin olive oil and sauté garlic until aromatic; mix in chicken broth and garbanzo beans until warmed through.
- Cook for 3 minutes, or until spinach has wilted, stirring occasionally.
- Place 1/6 of the sauce, peppercorns, and Parmesan on each dish.
- Immediately serve

Eggplant Steak with Feta Cheese, Black Olives, Roasted Peppers, and Chickpeas

Time to prepare: 10 minutes

Approximately 4 servings

Ingredients:

- Marinade balsamic
- 2 garlic cloves, minced
- 1 tbsp. tamari (low sodium) a tablespoon of balsamic vinegar
- freshly ground black pepper, quarter teaspoon 2 tbsp olive oil (extra virgin)
- Steaks of Eggplant
- 1 big eggplant (1 pound) 1/4 pound crumbled feta cheese 1 1/2 cups drained chickpeas 2 chopped roasted red peppers balsamic vinegar, 4 tsp oregano, a pinch
- half a cup black olives, pitted Sea salt
- black pepper, freshly ground 4 pita breads (6 1/2-inch circular) Garnish with fresh oregano

Directions::

- Prepare the marinade:
- Combine marinade ingredients in a mixing basin. Ingredients: Mix in extra virgin olive oil gradually until thoroughly blended.
- Place aside.
- Preheat the grill or broiler.

- Cut the eggplant lengthwise into 4 quarter-inch thick slices to resemble steaks.
- Brush the marinade over the eggplant slices and broil or grill until cooked, approximately 2 minutes each side.
- One by one, place the grilled eggplants on the plates.
- Combine feta, red peppers, chickpeas, oregano, and black olives in a small mixing bowl; season with sea salt and crushed black pepper.
- Stir in some marinade until completely combined.
- Pita bread should be grilled or toasted and sliced into wedges before serving.
- Drizzle balsamic vinegar over 2 scoops of the olive-pepper mixture over the eggplant "steak."
- Garnish with oregano sprigs and a couple pita bread slices. Continue with the remaining ingredients and serve right away.

Pasta with tomatoes and spinach.

Time to prepare: 25 minutes

Ingredients:

- 60g can tomatoes, drained 100g whole-wheat pasta 7.5ml extra virgin olive oil half onion, sliced 60g spinach, frozen
- 13 cup feta cheese, crumbled 1 tsp salt 1 tsp pepper

Directions:

- Cook pasta until al dente according to package directions in a saucepan of boiling water.

- Meanwhile, heat the oil in a pan over medium heat, then add the onion and cook for 3 minutes. Cook for approximately 10 minutes after adding the tomatoes.

- Cook until the spinach is cooked thoroughly.

- Drain the pasta and mix it with the sauce until it is well covered. Season with salt and pepper, then top with feta cheese.

Sauté with green beans and zucchini

Time to prepare: 10 minutes

Approximately 4 servings

Ingredients:

- 7.5ml extra virgin olive oil, split

- 50g green beans, trimmed and chopped into little pieces half a small zucchini, thinly sliced 2 tablespoons red chili flakes

- lemon juice (7.5 mL) 15g scallions, sliced 1 teaspoon red chili flakes

- a few flakes of parmesan 1 teaspoon pepper 1 teaspoon salt

Directions:

- In a medium-sized skillet, heat half of the oil.

- Stir in the green beans, zucchini, salt, and pepper, and cook for approximately 9 minutes, turning occasionally, until the veggies are crisp tender.

- Take the skillet off the heat and add the lemon juice and scallions. Serve with cheese and red chili flakes on top.

Dish with stuffed grape leaves.

1 hour 30 minutes to cook

Approximately 8 servings

Ingredients:

- 30 grape leaves, fresh
- 2 tbsp olive oil (extra virgin) 2 cups onion, finely diced
- brown rice, 1 cup
- 1 cup currants or raisins, dried 1 cup fresh mint, chopped
- 1 cup fresh parsley, chopped
- 1 cup hulled pistachios, chopped 1 gallon tomato juice
- to taste with sea salt and pepper Drizzle with pomegranate molasses
- quarter cup lemon juice, freshly squeezed 1 sliced lemon
- 1 tablespoon extra virgin olive oil for coating the casserole dish and the casserole's top

Directions:

- Cook for around 2 minutes in a kettle of boiling water before draining and setting aside.

- Heat extra virgin olive oil in a large saucepan over medium heat; add onion and sauté for approximately 10 minutes, or until gently browned.
- Bring the rice and 2 1/2 cups water to a moderate boil, then cover and lower to medium low heat.
- Cook for approximately 40 minutes, or until the rice is tender and the liquid has been absorbed.
- Remove the cooked rice from the fire and add the lemon juice, raisins, mint, parsley, pistachios, tomato juice, sea salt, and pepper to taste.
- Preheat the oven to 350 degrees Fahrenheit.
- Line the bottom of a 2-quart baking dish with grape leaves, allowing them to dangle over the edges, with extra virgin olive oil.
- Pat the leaves dry with paper towels and distribute half of the rice mixture on top.
- Add additional grape leaves to the rice mixture and finish with the remaining rice.
- Cover with the remaining leaves and seal the edges by folding the leaves over.
- Brush the top of the casserole with extra virgin olive oil and bake for approximately 40 minutes, or until the dish is firm and dry and the grape leaves have darkened.
- Cut the dish into eight pieces with a damp knife and serve on eight plates.
- Drizzle pomegranate molasses over each plate and top with lemon wedges.

Salsa with olives, bell peppers, and arugula.

Time to cook: 5 minutes

1 and a half cup

Ingredients:

- 1 tablespoon extra virgin olive oil 1 teaspoon fennel seeds, crushed
- 1 diced red and yellow bell pepper half cup chopped baby arugula 16 pitted Kalamata olives, diced Sea salt and pepper to taste

Directions:

- Heat extra virgin olive oil in a large nonstick pan and toss in fennel seeds for approximately 1 minute.
- Stir in the bell peppers and cook for another 4 minutes, or until they are tender.
- Scrape the pepper mixture into a mixing bowl, then add the olives, salt, and pepper.
- Allow flavors to mingle for at least 2 minutes, stirring regularly.
- Toss in the arugula until it is slightly wilted, then serve.

Dip with roasted peppers and beans

Time to cook: 0 minutes

2 half-cup yield

Ingredients:

- 1 jar roasted red bell peppers (7 oz.) 1 tablespoon olive oil (extra virgin)

- 1 cannellini bean (16 oz.) washed and drained 1 cup (6 oz.) light firm silken tofu garlic clove, minced half teaspoon ground cumin tbsp. lime juice
- 13 cup cilantro leaves 1/2 teaspoon salt

Directions:

- Place a quarter cup of roasted peppers aside.
- In a food processor, combine the leftover roasted peppers with the other ingredients and process until completely smooth.
- Transfer the pepper mixture to a serving dish and whisk in the saved peppers. Serve refrigerated or at room temperature.

Nachos with vegetables.

2 minute cook time

Approximately 6 servings

Ingredients:

- thinly sliced medium green onion (about 1 tbsp.) 1 tsp. oil from a package of sun-dried tomatoes 1 neatly sliced and drained plum tomato
- 2 tbsp. coarsely chopped sun-dried tomatoes in oil 2 tablespoons coarsely chopped Kalamata olives
- Corn tortilla chips, 4 oz., restaurant style
- 1 box finely crushed feta cheese (4 ounce)

Directions:

- In a small bowl, combine the onion, plum tomato, oil, sun-dried tomatoes, and olives; put aside.

- Arrange the tortilla chips in a single layer on a microwavable dish; equally top with cheese and microwave for 1 minute on high.

- Microwave for 30 seconds longer, or until the cheese is bubbling, after rotating the dish half a turn.

- Serve the tomato mixture over the chips and cheese in an even layer.

Boats made of jalapeos.

Time to prepare: 25 minutes.

Approximately 44 servings

Ingredients:

- 1 vegetarian burger crumbs (12 oz.) bag 1 cup shredded Parmesan cheese
- 1 package (8 oz) (8 oz.) light cream cheese, softened
- 22 jalapeño jalapenos, sliced lengthwise in half and seeds removed

Directions:

- In a large pan over medium heat, cook crumbles for approximately 5 minutes, or until cooked through.
- In a separate bowl, combine the grated Parmesan and softened cream cheese; fold in the crumble.
- Preheat oven to 425 degrees Fahrenheit. Fill each jalapeño half with approximately 1 tablespoon crumble-

cheese mixture; lay the jalapeno halves on a baking sheet, cheese side up, and bake for about 20 minutes, or until the filling is bubbling and lightly browned.

Potatoes from Greece.

2 hours to prepare.

Approximately 4 servings

Ingredients:

- one-quarter cup lemon juice
- 2 garlic cloves, finely chopped 1 and a half cup water
- 13 cup extra virgin olive oil
- a sprinkle of black pepper, ground 2 bouillon cubes (chicken)
- 1 teaspoon rosemary, dry 1 teaspoon thyme, dry
- 6 potatoes, peeled and quartered

Directions:

- Preheat the oven to 350 degrees Fahrenheit.
- In a small bowl, combine the lemon juice, garlic, water, olive oil, pepper, bouillon cubes, rosemary, and thyme.
- In a medium-sized baking dish, arrange the potatoes in a single layer and drizzle with the olive oil mixture.
- Cover and bake for approximately 2 hours or until tender, rotating twice.

Bites of stuffed celery

Approximately 8 servings

15-minute prep time

Ingredients:

- Cooking spray with olive oil 1 garlic clove, minced 2 tablespoons pine nuts
- 8 celery stalks quarter cup shredded Italian cheese mixture celery leaves 1 fat-free cream cheese (8 oz.)
- 2 tablespoons dry-roasted sunflower seeds

Directions:

- Coat a nonstick pan with olive oil cooking spray, then add the garlic and pine nuts and cook for 4 minutes over medium heat, or until golden brown.
- Place aside.
- To make a flat surface, cut off the broad base and tips of the celery and take two thin strips from the round side.
- In a mixing dish, combine Italian cheese and cream cheese; spread into celery and cut each stalk into 2-inch pieces.
- Cover and let aside for at least 4 hours before serving. Sprinkle half of the celery pieces with sunflower seeds and half with the pine nut mixture.

Mushrooms with Pesto.

Time to cook: 6 hours

Approximately 14 servings

Ingredients::

- 14+ cleaned and stemmed button mushrooms
- extra virgin olive oil, half cup 3 garlic cloves
- 2 tablespoons basil
- pine nuts (half cup) walnuts, 1 cup
- a half teaspoon of salt

Directions::

- Place the mushroom caps on a platter, top-side down.
- Combine stuffing ingredients in a food processor and pulse until smooth.
- Scoop an equal quantity of filling into each cap and dehydrate for 6 hours at 105°F until soft.
- Serve hot.

14-Day Meal Plan

DAY 1	Breakfast: **Paninis with cream.** Lunch: **Soup with Parsley.** Dinner: **Bruschetta with chicken.**
DAY 2	Breakfast: **Couscous for breakfast.** Lunch: **Delicious Lentil Soup** Dinner: **Chicken with Coconut.**
DAY 3	Breakfast: **Hash with potatoes and chickpeas.** Lunch: **Barley Soup with Veggies** Dinner: **Burgers with turkey.**
DAY 4	Breakfast: **Toast with avocado.** Lunch: **Soup with chickpeas** Dinner: **Greek Salad with Chicken**
DAY 5	Breakfast: **Pancakes with a Mediterranean flair.** Lunch: **Soup with Red Lentil Beans** Dinner: **Chicken Braised with Olives**
DAY 6	Breakfast: **Frittata Mediterranean.** Lunch: **Soup made with chickpeas and lentil beans.**

	Dinner: **Chicken Braised with Mushrooms and Olives**
DAY 7	Breakfast: **Oatmeal with Nutty Bananas.** Lunch: **Rotelle Soup with Fish** Dinner: **Olives, Mustard Greens, and Lemon Chicken**
DAY 8	Breakfast: **Omelet with Mediterranean Veggies** Lunch: **Soup with beans and cabbage.** Dinner: **Chicken from the Mediterranean.**
DAY 9	Breakfast: **Scones with lemon.** Lunch: **Soup de Minestrone** Dinner:
DAY 10	Breakfast: **Wrapped Breakfast** Lunch: **Soup with spicy lentils and spinach.** Dinner: **Salad with warm chicken and avocado.**
DAY 11	Breakfast: **Scrambled Eggs with Garlic.** Lunch: **Tomato Pesto Soup with Three Beans** Dinner: **Stew with chicken.**
DAY 12	Breakfast: **Breakfast Casserole with Fruit.** Lunch: **Soup with Lemon.**

	Dinner: **Roasted Vegetables with Chicken**
DAY 13	Breakfast: **Breakfast Casserole with Eggs and Sausage**
	Lunch: **Beef Stew with Red Wine from the Mediterranean.**
	Dinner: **Olive Relish on Grilled Chicken**
DAY 14	Breakfast: **Pancakes with Yogurt.**
	Lunch: **Chickpeas with Plum Tomatoes Chicken Stew**
	Dinner: **Turkey grilled with salsa**

Conclusion

It's generally known that people in Mediterranean nations live longer and suffer less from chronic illnesses like heart disease, cancer, and type 2 diabetes than the rest of the world. The Mediterranean diet is a way of life that emphasizes consuming fresh, healthful, and natural foods. Health and nutrition are the most important principles in life. Your first objective should always be to feed your body good food, and what better way to do so than with the Mediterranean diet?

This is the perfect moment to start if you've tried a thousand strategies to reduce weight without results. If you follow this plan, you will be several pounds lighter by the end of next week, due to this incredible diet—and week after week, you will be a healthier and lighter version of yourself. The delectable recipes in this book will help you make healthy eating a priority in your household, as well as provide opportunities for family enjoyment around mealtime.

Printed in Great Britain
by Amazon